INTO BROWN BEAR COUNTRY

INTO BROWN

BEAR COUNTRY

WILL TROYER

UNIVERSITY OF ALASKA PRESS
FAIRBANKS

University of Alaska Press
P.O. Box 756240
Fairbanks, AK 99775-6240
888-252-6657
907-474-5831
fypress@uaf.edu
www.uaf.edu/uapress

This paper meets the requirements of ANSI/NISO Z39.48-1992.

Library of Congress Cataloging-in-Publication Data

Troyer, Will (Willard A.)
    Into brown bear country / Will Troyer.
        p. cm.
    Includes bibliographical references.
    ISBN-13: 978-1-889963-72-3 (isbn 13 pbk. : alk. paper)
    ISBN-10: 1-889963-72-0 (isbn 10 pbk. : alk. paper)
  1. Brown bear—Alaska. I. Title.
    QL737.C27T77 2005
    599.784′09798–dc22
                                        2004029040

Cover design: Mike Kirk
Interior design: Dixon Jones, Rasmuson Library Graphics

For my family—

LuRue, Janice, Eric, and Teresa—

who kept the home fires burning

CONTENTS

ACKNOWLEDGMENTS

Many people aided me in my years of research on the Alaska brown bear. I am especially indebted to the field assistants who shared my frustrations, and sometimes danger, in my early work on Kodiak Island. Many thanks to Earl Fleming, a real old-timer who understood bears, and Ken Durley, Stephen Browne, Ken Howell, Howard Chrest, and Dick Hensel, without whose help and dedication I could never have developed a livetrapping method bears or gathered the research data that followed. Dick Hensel's sense of humor got us through many discouraging days.

Dave Spencer, my supervisor for nineteen years, believed in my efforts and gave me support and encouragement for some of my pioneering efforts even when some of my projects and plans must have looked hopeless and precarious to him. Personnel at the Alaska Department of Fish and Game who assisted at Katmai were Jim Faro, Al Franzman, Chuck Swartz, Larry Aumiller, Dick Russell, Chris Smith, Cindy Zabel, and Fred Deciese. I thank them. I am especially grateful to Sterling Miller (formerly with the Alaska Department of Fish and Game), Larry Van Daele, Tom Smith, and an anonymous reader who reviewed the entire manuscript and offered many valuable suggestions. I sincerely appreciate the efforts of John Schoen and Dick Hensel, who read various chapters and added their insights.

I am indebted to the National Park Service personnel who aided in searching for darted bears: Rollie Ostermick, Libby Mills, Mary Weber, Jeff Moody, Bruce Kaye, and Mike Tollefson. Thanks also to Gil Blinn, park superintendent, and Bob Peterson, assistant regional director, who always managed to fund my efforts when money was scarce.

A special debt is owed to Martin Grosnick, my summer field assistant at Katmai, who shared many an exciting moment as we stalked brown bears with a Cap-chur gun.

Michael Parks and Lydia Rabottini persuaded me to join their team and become a guide/naturalist aboard the vessel *Waters*. It permitted me to spend many hours eyeball to eyeball with bears and learn more of the intricate behavior of this unique animal. Thanks, Mike and Lydia. I am privileged to have met the many clients who shared those wonderful days afield.

The book was molded into its final form with valuable comments from my dedicated literary agent Jeanne Fredericks and the editorial staff at the University of Alaska Press, Erica Hill and Jennifer Collier. Jennifer's editing was first-rate.

Thanks to the many friends who encouraged me to write this book. My son Eric offered much appreciated advice on the manuscript, and special thanks go to my wife LuRue, who spent hours editing and making suggestions on each chapter. Without her efforts, I doubt the project would have been completed.

INTRODUCTION

I had followed a well-worn bear trail for several hours to reach the headwaters of the Sturgeon River. As I walked along the edge of the stream, dozens of chum salmon skittered through the shallow riffles. Others were digging redds in which to lay their eggs. The remains of several fish lay on a small mud bar, surrounded by numerous bear tracks. When I heard the loud splashing of a bear chasing salmon, I stopped in time to see the bear come into view around a bend in the river. As soon as the animal became aware of my presence, it rose on its hind legs to peer at me. We stood quietly staring at one another for a full minute before the large bear dropped to all fours and galloped into a thick patch of willows.

I continued downstream and climbed a ridge. Scanning several forks of the Sturgeon with my binoculars, I spotted six more bears chasing salmon and a family of three descending a mountain. On a small knoll across the river, a female brown bear lay on her back as her three cubs suckled contentedly. Bald eagles and gulls wheeled in the sky. It was the wild, primordial scene that I had dreamt about in my youth. I was alone, but far from lonely, in this breathtakingly vast wilderness.

My interest in brown bears was kindled at an early age. Bored with the hard work and monotonous life on an Indiana farm, I read extensively of adventure, exploration, and exotic animals in more interesting parts of the world.

One winter in my early teens I came across J. M. Holzworth's book *The Wild Grizzlies of Alaska* about Alan Hasselborg, a recluse who lived in a remote bay on Admiralty Island. Brown bears were his only neighbors. The book was filled with Hasselborg's adventures and association with the giant beasts as he hiked through the wild rain forest. It was also sprinkled with black-and-white photos of the bears.

I was spellbound with Hasselborg's life, the massive bears, and the description of the remote wilderness. I read the book several times by the light of a kerosene lamp. I vowed that someday I too would go live among the brown bears.

Soon after I arrived in Southeast Alaska in the early 1950s, I found myself at Mole Harbor on Admiralty Island. Hasselborg's cabin stood at the edge of the rain forest, tucked back in the little bay. The cabin was empty; Hasselborg had left the area a few years before because of ill health. But the brown bears were still there, feeding on salmon that were spawning in the stream near the cabin. The forest was interlaced with a network of bear trails.

During my three years in Southeast Alaska with the U.S. Fish and Wildlife Service, I encountered many brown bears and began to admire and respect these noble animals. In the 1950s predatory animals in Alaska were relentlessly pursued and destroyed by individuals as well as agencies. The federal government had recently removed the bounty on bald eagles, making it illegal to shoot them, but few people honored the new law. Some commercial fishermen shot bears indiscriminately because they competed for salmon. A territorial agency dynamited sea lion rookeries for the same reason. A predator control division of the U.S. Fish and Wildlife Service shot and poisoned wolves and killed seals. The territory placed bounties on wolves, wolverines, and seals. The fledgling livestock industry had a tenuous foothold in Alaska and considered bears a detriment to the raising of cattle—some people were advocating bounties on brown bears as well.

The prevailing attitude was that whatever competed with humans should be eliminated. At that time I could not foresee that, in a few decades, multitudes of people would travel to Alaska just to see bears and other wildlife that had been so long maligned.

In 1955 I became refuge manager of the Kodiak National Wildlife Refuge, a two-million-acre reserve that had been set aside for brown bears in 1941. I still remember my first flight over Kodiak Island. Bear trails crisscrossed the grassy landscape that was interspersed with willow, alder, and elderberry thickets. It was quite a contrast to the rain forests of Southeast Alaska.

I remarked to the pilot that this bear country was going to be a snap to walk through compared to the devil's club–infested forests of the Southeast. I would later find that those nice grassy meadows

that I was viewing from the air contained vegetation that was well over my head, and the alder thickets were often a jungle of branches that I could traverse only by crawling through them on my hands and knees.

Soon after my arrival at Kodiak, I recognized the need for some basic biological studies on brown bears. Little scientific information was available. Everyone knew that bears ate salmon and berries, grazed on many plants, grew large, and hibernated in the winter. But much more was unknown. How many bears were there on Kodiak? At what age did they attain full growth? How old did they get? At what age did they first breed? How many cubs could a sow produce during her lifetime?

We needed answers to these questions and many more in order to understand how a brown bear population functioned. Guides were luring more and more hunters to Kodiak; guiding had become a lucrative business. What effect was hunting having on the population? Were bear numbers increasing, decreasing, or stable?

I recognized that we would have many obstacles to overcome before we could undertake a study. No one had developed a method of capturing and marking the Alaska brown bears. I knew that this was a key to gathering scientific data. Little money was available for such a project; my total annual budget for managing the entire refuge was $8,000. Modern technology had not yet arrived; radio collars, Cap-chur guns, and adequate drugs for immobilizing bears were still methods of the future. Being a young, ambitious biologist, however, I plunged ahead with the project.

One modern development that was available was the airplane. I soon saw the advantage of flying over bear country to count the animals and gather other data. I could glean information in a few hours of flying that would have taken weeks to accomplish on foot. Hence, early in my career I learned to fly small airplanes.

During my eight years on Kodiak Island, from 1955 to 1963, my summer field assistants and I pioneered techniques for livetrapping brown bears. We captured and released nearly two hundred bears during these years. We began to gather the basic biological information necessary to understand these unique animals.

Today biologists are conducting studies on brown bears throughout Alaska. They have a variety of sophisticated technological equipment and techniques at their disposal. This has resulted in the publication of reams of scientific information on brown bears. Professional and amateur photographers with modern camera equipment also seek out bears in every corner of Alaska; their beautiful photographs grace the covers and pages of magazines and books. Yes, the public has started to learn about, learned to appreciate, the brown bear.

After I left Kodiak in 1963, I spent a decade in other parts of Alaska working with other species of mammals and birds. In 1974 I returned to my first love, the brown bear. I initiated studies on the bears of Katmai National Park for the National Park Service. This gave me an opportunity to work with a different population of brown bears in another region of Alaska. I continued these studies through 1981, when I retired.

In the 1990s I became involved in guiding small groups of photographers and bear watchers along the Katmai Coast. This work gave me additional opportunities to spend hours in close proximity to bears, observing their habits and interactions.

I gained new insights into the behavior of brown bears that I did not have time to pursue while working as a biologist.

Many of my clients have quizzed me relentlessly about brown bears. How big do they get? When do they breed? How far do they travel? Where do they hibernate? What do they eat? How well can they see, hear, smell, and so forth? Half a century after I began collecting data on bears, a lot of scientific information is indeed available, but there continues to be a major need to synthesize this information and present it in a form that is interesting and accessible to the general public. That is the major goal of this book—to provide biological information without losing readers in scientific jargon. I also hope people will come to understand bears as the enchanting creatures they are, in contrast to the ferocious killer so often depicted in popular literature.

A second motive is to record some of the attitudes and conflicts that arose between bears and people in the early years in Alaska. Conflicts between bears and salmon and between bears and cattle are now history, but they should not be forgotten. As human population grows and expands, wildlife habitat will inevitably shrink and other conflicts will arise. But the continued existence of our wilderness neighbors is essential, not only for our pleasure but also for the delicate balance of nature that sustains our planet.

Lastly, my experiences in pioneering the early bear studies in Alaska have been a source of entertainment during many evenings over a social cup of coffee. I have received numerous requests to record these adventures on paper.

I hope I have accomplished these goals.

FIGURE 1   *A mother and cub digging clams on the shore of Hallo Bay, Katmai National Park.*

MEET THE BROWN BEAR

POWERFUL SHOULDER MUSCLES RIPPLED WITH EACH *methodical step as the giant brown bear strode down the trail. His dark brown fur, wet from the morning dew, glistened in the low rays of the morning sun. Following the trail to the top of a small hill, he rose to his hind legs to survey the landscape. His head swung slowly from side to side as his penetrating eyes scrutinized the horizon. The bear knew that he was king of his domain and had little to fear in his surroundings.*

Bears are the most revered animals in North America. Numerous legends and myths surround them; gross exaggerations of their habits and feats are the rule rather than the exception.

The first time I met a brown bear, I knew little about the animal beyond overblown tales of its ferociousness. New to the territory of Alaska, which was to become a state in 1959, I was hiking across the tidal flats of a saltwater bay in Southeast Alaska. A light drizzle fell as I followed the edge of a tidal channel. Through the rainy mist, the movement of an animal behind a huge drift log caught my eye. As I stopped to get a better look, a brown bear planted both front feet on the log, its nose high in the air. It was still more than 150 yards away, but it appeared enormous and the brownie had obviously spotted me. I stood, staring back, not knowing what to expect as some of the old tales flashed through my mind. The bear decided to investigate further and came running across the open flats. It stopped about seventy-five yards away and stood on its hind legs to get a better view. I looked for an escape route, but saw none; I took little comfort in the thirty-foot tidal channel that still separated us. The bear dropped to all four feet and ambled forward until it was directly across the channel. Then it rose on its hind legs to peer at me once more.

I know now that it was trying to determine what creature had invaded its territory, but at the time I was convinced I was about to be its victim. We stood there eyeball to eyeball for a very long minute. An old-timer had told me to talk to bears when they got too close, and I began telling the animal in my most soothing voice to please leave, that I meant it no harm. Facing the bear, I was lonely and just plain scared. My voice must have quavered as I kept up the monologue, for I knew that if it decided to cross the channel and attack, I didn't have a chance. Then a light breeze drifted across the water, and the bear got a good whiff of my scent. The bear snorted, dropped to all fours, and galloped away. I sat down on a log, wiped the sweat from my brow, and watched it disappear into the forest.

This encounter began a new chapter in my lifelong fascination with these huge animals, the largest living land carnivores in North America. I became a keen observer of the brown bears, intrigued by their habits and behavior. In later years as a research biologist, I studied them extensively to learn more about the biological puzzles that surround them and their environment. Secrets about the bears continue to unravel; they are complex animals. Like humans, each is an individual; no two react the same way. The brown bear has become a controversial animal because people tend to generalize the behavior of all bears from an extraordinary, and usually negative, experience with one individual.

Controversy also seems to surround them in the scientific field. In 1918 scientist C. Hart Merriam divided the North American brown and grizzly bears into eighty-six forms based on slight variations in color, size, and skull shape. He gave little consideration to the fact that physical differences exist in small populations and even within family groups. Since then, various scientists have rejected Dr. Merriam's work.

After an extensive study of skulls, Dr. Robert L. Rausch in 1963 classified all North American browns and grizzlies, along with the Eurasian brown bears, into the single species *Ursus arctos*. Most scientists have since followed this classification. Rausch did feel, however, that the brown bears on Kodiak and nearby islands varied enough from other North American bears that they should be considered a separate subspecies, so he classified the Kodiak bears as *Ursus arctos middendorffi*. All other grizzlies and brown bears were then listed into the subspecies *Ursus arctos horribilis*. These two are the only subspecies of brown and grizzly bears currently recognized in North America. Various DNA studies on brown and grizzly bears now under way, however, may again change the taxonomy of bears and result in the recognition of additional subspecies.

Regardless of this technical scientific distinction in North America, the popular name for the bear in interior Alaska has long been *grizzly*, whereas the Alaska coastal bear is known as the *brown bear*. Some argue that since they are the same species, they ought to be given the same common name; these advocates have applied the name *brown-grizzly*, adding more confusion. Others believe that the differences in size, behavior, and coloration justify different categories. The coastal brown bears do, in fact, grow much larger than the interior grizzlies. This is probably due to a better and more plentiful food supply rather than to a genetic variation. Some think that grizzlies are more aggressive than brown bears. I tend to agree with this belief, but I must admit that the aggressive behavior of the grizzlies may result more from a relationship to their environment than from an inherent modification in temperament.

No definite geographic line separates the two types, and in fact the brown bears' range gradually joins that of the grizzlies toward its inland boundary. The Boone and Crockett Club, for the sake of separating records of brown bears from those of interior grizzlies, uses the Alaska Range as a dividing line. Andy Russell, in his book *Grizzly Country*, refers to this rule and humorously states that a brown bear can walk up a pass from the south and, as it crosses the divide, become a grizzly.

FIGURE 2   *Skulls were used to classify all brown and grizzly bears of the world as one species,* Ursus arctos.

In spite of this controversy, I feel it would be a shame to have the popularly known brown bear called a grizzly and vice versa. Since we cannot separate their range geographically by exact lines, we cannot always distinguish between them. The same situation exists with many species of birds and mammals that are given a common name in one region but are known by a completely different name in another part of the country. Local traditions always seem to prevail. Kodiak Islanders have long called the brown bear the Kodiak bear; in Europe *Ursus arctos* is known as the European brown bear. I find no fault with this.

This book is about the *coastal* brown bear. The brown bear is a handsome animal and extremely bulky, with powerful muscles that cover its massive, dense bones and give it great strength. Its ears are short and rounded, set apart by the broad forehead. Its tail is short and is usually concealed by hair.

FIGURE 3   *Brown bears have a pronounced shoulder hump that distinguishes them from black bears.*

The brown bear is slightly more dish-faced than the black bear. Its brown eyes are small compared to its large muzzle; its nose is black. Its lips are charcoal-colored, hairless at the margins, and tend to droop loosely over its jaws. One rarely sees the lips curled back into the snarl that is so often depicted in mounted specimens. Taxidermists mount them in this fashion to show ferocity, but the pose is deceptive.

The brown bear, like the grizzly, has an obvious shoulder hump, which distinguishes it readily in the field from the black bear. The front claws also serve as a field characteristic in separating the two species. The black bear's claws are always less than two inches long whereas the brown bear's claws are often as long as four inches. Some claws are dark brown; others are creamy or ivory-colored. Claws tend to turn white with age, but I have seen young bears with beautiful cream-colored claws.

The color of the coastal brown bear is some shade of brown, light to dark, with the females tending to be lighter than the males. Color variation is considerable; fairly blond animals often have dark littermates. Its legs are usually darker than the body. Cubs frequently have a white band around the neck and shoulder, which gives them the appearance of wearing a collar. They may retain this band for some time, but it gradually diminishes with age; one rarely sees collars in bears over three years of age.

FIGURE 4   *Brown bears have long claws that tend to turn lighter with age.*

FIGURE 5   *The brown bear's hair color varies from dark brown to creamy.*

FIGURE 6   *Brown bears rub on logs and other objects to help shed their coats in the summer.*

All brown bears undergo a shedding period. This may start in the spring, but it is more commonly under way during the summer and complete by early September. During the shedding period, bears spend considerable time rubbing on trees, rocks, shrubs, and other objects to remove the long guard hairs. This apparently satisfies an itch. They will stand with their backs against a tree, rubbing up and down or across. They often choose lone trees. Even where trees are plentiful, a bear may pick out one specific tree and use it repeatedly. These rubbing trees are easy to spot in bear country; the bark is rubbed smooth, and bear hairs hang profusely on the tree trunk and along projecting limbs.

Claw marks are also apparent on these trees. Bears stretch their full length and claw as high as they can reach, much as a domestic cat claws a post. Many people believe that bears do this to let others know how large they are and to establish their claims to an area. I have never seen any confirmation of this theory and I believe it is simply a habit of a bear stretching as high as it can reach.

As the rubbing removes the guard hairs, bears begin to appear unkempt and tattered in contrast to their beautiful glossy appearance in a full new coat. Hunters refer to such animals as "rubbed" bears and consider them unsuitable for a trophy. Some bears emerge from hibernation with rubbed spots. I suspect that just prior to the time

FIGURE 7   *This cub at Brooks Camp on Naknek Lake, Katmai National Park, displays a characteristic white collar that usually disappears at around three years of age.*

they leave the den, they rub themselves on objects within the den.

Those who have never met a brown bear in the wild have yet to experience one of nature's most magnificent moments. Imagine the sight, at close range, of a large bear standing on its hind legs, a bear family sleeping on a serene knoll, or two large, angry bears confronting one another in the middle of a salmon stream. For those who love wild nature, encountering the brown bear under such circumstances is the only way to be introduced to this mighty animal.

FIGURE 8   *A large, dark male feeds on sedges on a tidal flat at Kukak Bay in Katmai National Park.*

2

BEAR COUNTRY

One evening in late July on Kodiak Island, a *reddish glow crept across the western sky as the sun disappeared behind the mountains. The wind was abating after a blustery day. As the evening shadows lengthened, the stormy waters of Karluk Lake turned placid. The rustling of the alder leaves ceased, and in the distance I could hear the faint, flutelike notes of a hermit thrush. All became still, except for the raucous calls of a group of gulls fighting over a dead salmon. Several arctic terns flew low along the lakeshore with jerky wing beats, while two bald eagles soared high in the sky. Another sat quietly on a dead cottonwood snag, guarding its young in the nearby nest.*

I had spent several hours that morning climbing through thick alder brush to reach my panoramic perch.

9

FIGURE 9   *The Karluk Lake drainage within the Kodiak National Wildlife Refuge contains optimal bear habitat. It has many high mountain slopes suitable for denning and a variety of food resources such as salmon, elderberries, and other vegetation. Willow and alder thickets provide cover for hiding. The south side of Karluk Lake is in the foreground, with O'Malley River and O'Malley Lake beyond it.*

Craggy three-thousand-foot peaks, separated by a green valley, dominated the landscape. Canyon Creek rushed out of the mountains, cascading down the steep ravines before it wound a serpentine course to Karluk Lake far below me. In the distance O'Malley River flowed out of a crystal-clear lake that was nestled in the southeastern end of the valley. It meandered for a mile before joining Canyon Creek near its terminus. Both waterways were filled with spawning salmon. Alder and elderberry thickets covered the mountain slopes; groves of tall cottonwood trees were scattered here and there at lower

elevations. Interspersed among the trees and shrubs were meadows of tall grass and fireweed.

Tying this landscape together was a maze of bear trails. Like a huge spiderweb, the trails crisscrossed the valley floor, weaving in and around alder thickets and cottonwood groves. For thousands of years, bears had trodden these trails and, in places, worn them two feet deep. From previous visits, I knew that forty to fifty bears fed in this small valley during the salmon spawning season. They fattened up on the protein-rich fish and supplemented their diet with berries that grew luxuriantly throughout the area. I had decided to spend a few days at this observation point with my binoculars, watching bears feed and interact with each other. Very soon the big brown bears would be leaving their day beds in the alders and moving to the streams to feed. I had done this many times before, never tiring of the drama.

Before long, two subadults came ambling down a trail and crossed the valley. As they approached the O'Malley River they started to run, anticipating a delicious meal. Leaping into the river with a splash, they immediately began pursuing several fleeing salmon through a shallow riffle. A half mile downriver, a large, dark boar emerged from the vegetation onto the riverbank. His broad head, low-slung belly, and rippling shoulder muscles indicated to me that he was a bear of stature in bear society. He moved slowly and methodically along the riverbank and then stepped onto a gravel bar. Like a gentleman going to dinner, he sat down for a few moments, eyeing the menu. Rising, he walked to the edge of the pool, paused again briefly, and then, quick as a flash, he pounced on a salmon. He grasped the flapping fish between his teeth, strolled to a nearby bank, and began to rip red flesh from the still-struggling salmon.

Other bears began appearing in the valley. A sow with three cubs and a single bear fished below the falls on Canyon Creek. Another sow with two yearlings came down a steep mountain slope, while in a large, grassy meadow three young bears playfully wrestled. Dinnertime had come to brown bear valley and I had twenty-one bears in view.

I watched the evening parade of bears for some time as the light gently faded. The early diners were leaving with their bellies full of salmon while newcomers were still arriving. Darkness eventually enveloped me, and I followed the night action by ear. Rapid splashes told me of bears chasing salmon; now and then a throaty growl signified a conflict in the bear world. The action would continue into the night as it had for hundreds of years in this wild valley filled with bears.

This was prime bear country, some of the best in Alaska.

The brown bears of Alaska are distributed over a vast coastal arc, stretching from the rain forests of Southeast Alaska to Kuskokwim Bay. They are found in the greatest numbers, however, in parts of Southeast Alaska, on Kodiak Island, and on the Alaska Peninsula.

In Southeast Alaska the brown bear inhabits most of the mainland coast north of Frederick Sound. There the bears reach their greatest numbers in the ABC islands: Admiralty, Baranof, and Chichagof. Biologists estimate that 1,500 to 1,700 brown bears live on the 1,709 square miles of Admiralty Island alone.

The ABC islands are characterized by rugged topography, with peaks rising several thousand feet high within a mile or less of the saltwater. The islands have many long bays, the sides of which rise steeply out of the water. Sedges, grasses, skunk cabbage, and other small plants grow abundantly along the many bays and deltas. A rain forest of Sitka spruce, western hemlock, and cedar, with an understory of devil's club, huckleberry, salmon-berry, mosses, and other plants covers the lower elevations. A little higher, the forest is sprinkled with bogs and muskegs; above timberline, alpine meadows of mountain heather, blueberry, crow-berry, Labrador tea, and other plants are common. Numerous streams drain these islands. Brown bears use the shorelines heavily in the spring to feed on the newly emerged vegetation. In the sum-mer they take migrating salmon from the water-ways; in the fall the alpine areas provide berries and denning sites.

In Prince William Sound in southcentral Alaska, the brown bears occupy Montague, Hinchinbrook, and Hawkins islands, but they are not found on many of the smaller islands. Brown bears are not abundant in the Cook Inlet region near Anchorage or on the Kenai Peninsula. Here, civilization has already crowded these large animals, forcing them out or greatly reducing their numbers.

From Cook Inlet, the great Alaska Peninsula juts southwest for five hundred miles, separating the Gulf of Alaska from the Bering Sea. In this area the large bears again reach some of their greatest densities; it includes the popular McNeil River Bear Sanctuary and Katmai National Park. Brown bears are found over the entire peninsula and on Unimak Island, the first island in the Aleutian Chain, but they are absent from the rest of the Aleutian Islands.

The interior and the southeastern side of the Alaska Peninsula are dominated by the lofty moun-tains of the Aleutian Range, which run the entire length of the peninsula and include various active and inactive volcanoes. Much of the northwestern side is a broad, flat coastal plain that stretches from the mountain foothills to the sandy beaches of the Bering Sea. A great number of meandering rivers, marshes, and small lakes carve the coastal plain. The vegetation contains stands of grass, sedges, heather, and a variety of other plants including cranberries, crowberries, blueberries, and an array of colorful wildflowers. Low willow and alder thickets dot the landscape, and in some areas sand dunes and lava beds are prominent. Mountain slopes on the eastern side of the peninsula recede directly to the ocean, often covered by dense stands of alders in addition to the usual heather, berries, and other vegetation. Only the northern part of the peninsula is sparsely covered with spruce, some birch, and balsam poplar trees.

High winds, fog, rain, and overcast skies are common in the summer due to a temperate cli-mate. Bears tend to use the mountains for denning, but in the spring they often travel to the coast of the Bering Sea to feed on new plants and search the beaches for marine mammals that may have washed ashore. The streams and rivers flowing out of the peninsula serve as spawning grounds for the greatest red salmon fishery in the world. During the summer months, bears concentrate in the shallow streams among the mountain foothills to feed on fish. In the fall they tend to return to the coastal plain in search of berries, late-spawning fish, and whatever they can glean before returning to the mountains to den.

Brown bears occupy the entire Bristol Bay region, but dwindle in numbers north and west to the Kuskokwim River and beyond. The milder climate of the southern coast gradually fades into these harsh arctic regions. Shorter seasons, less vegetation, and few salmon mean a reduced food supply for bears, in contrast to the fertile southern coastal regions. This zone is one of the gray areas

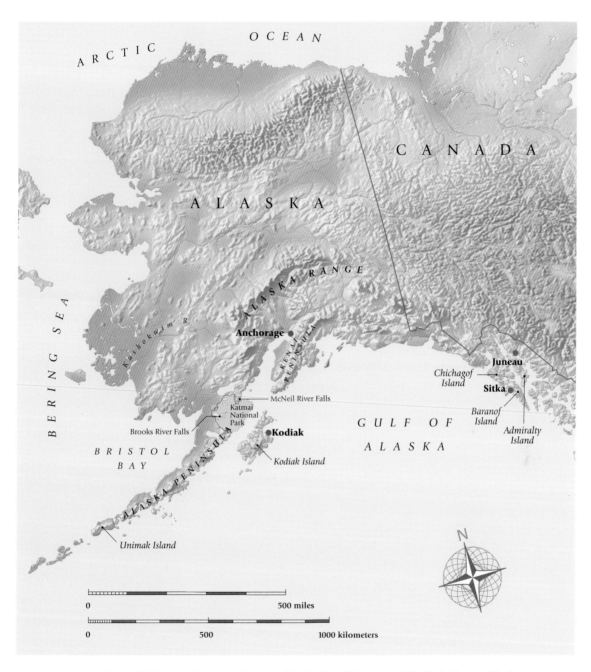

FIGURE 10   *Brown bears inhabit the southern coastal regions of Alaska. Bears living north of the Alaska Range, while the same species, are typically referred to as grizzly bears. The base map was reproduced from Mountain High Maps,® ©1993 Digital Wisdom, Inc.*

FIGURE 11   *The Valley of Ten Thousand Smokes provides little vegetation for bears nearly a century after the 1912 Katmai eruption.*

FIGURE 12   *An aerial view of the extensive sedge flats near the Swikshak River that are an important food source for bears in Katmai.*

where the range of the coastal brown bear dissolves into that of the northern and interior grizzly.

Brown bears inhabit all of Kodiak Island and some of the smaller nearby islands, including Afognak, Shuyak, Raspberry, and Uganik. Kodiak Island itself is 103 miles long and 57 miles wide, with deep, fjordlike bays. Rain and high-velocity winds often batter its rugged, thousand-mile coastline, which is also inhabited by sea lions, harbor seals, bald eagles, and thousands of seabirds. Scientists estimate that approximately 2,500 bears reside on the island.

The beauty of this land is seen in its lofty mountains, lush verdant valleys, and sparkling lakes and streams filled with salmon during summer and fall. Much of Afognak, Shuyak, Raspberry, and the northern part of Kodiak Island are covered with spruce forests. The remainder of Kodiak is basically treeless, with the exception of scattered groves of cottonwood trees and Kenai birches. Only on the southern portion of the island are the mountains lower, and a heathlike tundra persists in many places. Large meadows of grasses, sedges, and fireweed cover extensive areas, and in summer they give the appearance of great green pastures. These fields are strewn with dense stands of alders and willows. The alpine areas provide an abundance of crowberries, blueberries, and low-bush cranberries, whereas at the lower elevations elderberries and salmonberries grow profusely.

Kodiak Island, the Alaska Peninsula, and the ABC islands of Southeast Alaska support the largest populations of coastal brown bears in North America. The three geographic areas are different in many ways, but they do have similar features that provide ideal conditions for the great Alaska brown bears.

The entire coastal area has a maritime climate that produces mild temperatures, a plentiful supply of rain, and a long growing season compared to that of interior Alaska. This combination results in an abundance of vegetation. Tasty shoots and roots are available for spring feeding, and a variety of berries relished by bears ripen in the summer and fall. A number of rivers and streams drain the rain-soaked land and teem with spawning salmon during the summer and fall, providing a rich protein resource for the bears. All three areas are mountainous with brushy slopes that provide excellent cover and denning habitat.

Perhaps the most important ingredient is wild country. Wherever one finds a healthy population of brown bears, one also finds wild, uninhabited land. The brown bears, like the grizzlies, are wilderness animals; immense, unspoiled areas are as essential to their survival as are the succulent shoots, berries, and fish upon which they feed.

FIGURE 13   *A mother and cub at Hallo Bay, Katmai National Park.*

3
GROWING UP

FROST CRYSTALS CLUNG TO THE EDGES OF ALDER AND *willow leaves, covering also the grass and fireweed meadows that dotted the shores of Karluk Lake. The icy white landscape heralded the winter that was soon to follow.*

Far up on the mountain, Scarface, a large adult boar, was bedded in an alder thicket. At the first rays of light he got up, stretched, shook himself, and started to descend. His rich, dark-colored coat of fur contrasted sharply with the silvery wilderness. The frost shattered and fell to the ground as his body brushed against the stems and leaves; his trail became plainly visible as he moved down the mountain.

He arrived at the shores of Karluk Lake and, as the big bear stepped into the shallow water, spawning red salmon scooted for the depths. The back of one lingering salmon protruded above the surface and in a flash the bear had the first fish of the day clenched firmly in his teeth. He returned to a nearby meadow to feast on his catch. Placing his foot on the head of the flopping fish, he ripped and gulped down mouthfuls of flesh. Crimson blood stains dotted the frosty meadow. As he returned to the lake for another salmon, gulls dove from the sky and began to feed on the remains. During the course of this October morning, Scarface would continue along the shoreline, catching and eating twelve salmon before his hunger was sated.

Ever since the reds had arrived in the streams along Karluk Lake in early July, he had been gorging himself on the protein-rich salmon as well as on berries and various plants. He had gained weight at the rate of three pounds a day. His deep belly and fleshed-out legs and shoulders attested to the body fat that lay under his skin. He needed this surplus fat to sustain him during the long period of hibernation that was soon to come. He was a huge bear of approximately 1,200 pounds—a sharp contrast to his birth weight of one pound nearly ten years ago.

—————————————

No feature of a bear brings more inquiries from bear watchers than the size of the animal. The first questions I hear from people observing bears at close range are usually: How big is it? How long does it take for a bear to get that big? How much does it weigh? How big is

the bear that left that track? A large bear's huge body is an impressive sight for both seasoned observers and novice bear viewers.

To gain insight into the physical size and growth rate of bears, my assistants and I weighed and measured 162 individual brown bears on Kodiak Island in my early days of bear research. These varied in age from small cubs to full-grown adults. Most of these were captured in July and early August when they were feeding heavily on salmon and expanding rapidly in physical size as they accumulated excess fat to sustain themselves during hibernation. We then recaptured some in the late fall and during subsequent years to get information on individual physical growth over a given period of time.

Like Scarface, all brown bears are born in the winter den during January or February. They enter the world blind and naked, weighing only one pound. They grow rapidly on their mother's rich milk and by the time they leave the den in late May they are fourteen to sixteen pounds of bouncing energy. The small cubs continue to suckle, supplementing their milk diet with succulent plants and early salmon or other prey that their mother may catch. By mid-July they weigh forty-five pounds or more. In October or November, when they again enter the winter den with their mother, the cubs may exceed one hundred pounds. Some of this fall gain, however, is due to accumulated fat rather than growth.

By their second summer, as yearlings, cubs weigh around 135 pounds. In their third year of life, at the age of two and one-half, the males start to outgrow the females. In my research, I found that females of this age weighed from 105 to over 300 pounds, averaging 212 pounds. Males of this age varied from 155 to 310, averaging 225 pounds.

The rapid growth that occurs in the first few years of life begins to slow after the third summer.

FIGURE 14   *Cubs weigh about one pound when born in the winter den but grow rapidly. These six-month-old cubs in the Swikshak River marsh area in Katmai National Park each weigh approximately fifty to sixty pounds.*

Females reach their full adult size at about five years, when they weigh from 350 to 550 pounds in midsummer. Males, however, continue to grow, gaining about one hundred pounds per year until they reach full adulthood in eight to ten years. They usually weigh anywhere from five hundred to one thousand pounds. Exceptional individuals, such as Scarface, may tip the scales at well over one thousand when fully grown and carrying a heavy layer of fat.

After reaching maturity, both sexes continue to have seasonal physical changes. They accumulate considerable fat during the summer if food is abundant, reaching maximum physical bulk in the late fall. They live on their fat reserves during hibernation and gradually lose it. This loss continues in the spring after they emerge from the den when food supplies are still limited. Once they start feeding on a plentiful supply of vegetation, berries, and fish, the renewed storage of body fat reserves can be astounding.

If the food supply is plentiful, it is not unusual for adult sows to weigh only 350 pounds in early July and gain 150 pounds or more by mid-October. They become "butter fat" after a summer of gorging on salmon; they literally waddle when they walk. Fat depth on the rump of an adult male can be in excess of six inches.

The largest sow that we ever weighed was 660 pounds; the largest boar was an astounding 1,346 pounds. He was extremely fat and ready for hibernation. A large, fat adult male could possibly achieve

FIGURE 15   *Yearling cubs weigh approximately 135 pounds in their second summer, around eighteen months of age.*

FIGURE 16   *An adult male may exceed one thousand pounds, while mature females rarely weigh over five hundred pounds. This large male weighs approximately one thousand pounds.*

a weight of 1,500 pounds, but I doubt that any brown bear ever reached 2,000 pounds, as some people have suggested.

Young animals also gain rapidly; this spurt is the result of both physical growth and fat accumulation. One three-year-old male gained 45 pounds in 12 days, an increase of 3.7 pounds per day. Of course, part of this gain could have been the difference between an empty stomach when first captured and a full stomach twelve days later. Another three-year-old male weighed 335 pounds, but when recaptured seventy days later, he tipped the scales at 460—an increase of 125 pounds, or an average daily gain of 1.8 pounds.

In addition to weight, researchers take other measurements to calculate the growth rate and body size of bears. These include total length (distance between the tip of the nose and tip of the tail), body girth (taken behind the shoulder), hind foot length (distance between the back of the foot pad and the longest claw), hind foot and front foot widths (widest distance across the foot pad), shoulder height, and skull length and width.

The age at which different body parts become fully developed varies. Just like teenage boys, who reach adult height before they fill out, bears obtain their total length and height before their full bulk. Young bears, especially males, appear lean and lanky.

The skull is the last skeletal part to reach full maturity. Females reach maximum skull growth at about eight years and males at ten to twelve years of age. Biologists usually take skull measurements with a large set of calipers. The sum of the maximum length plus the maximum width reflects the size of the skull. Thus, a skull sixteen inches long by ten inches wide is referred to as a twenty-six-inch skull. The skull size is usually indicative of the physical mass of the animal. That is why hunters now use the skull measurement to rate the trophy value of a bear. Sometimes large old boars have a thirty-inch skull. The world-record skull, from a bear taken on Kodiak Island, is 30.75 inches. The skull size of females rarely exceeds twenty-five inches. If you find a skull in bear country and it measures more than twenty-six inches, it is safe to assume that it belongs to a large male.

Scientists have developed a method of aging bears by extracting a tooth (a small residual premolar) that has virtually no effect on the bear's ability to bite or to chew. A cross-section of a tooth reveals rings, similar to annual growth rings in trees, that can be counted to determine age.

The bear's feet are also indicative of the size of an individual bear. Bears often leave firm footprints on mudflats or sandbars. By measuring these tracks, one can roughly judge the size of the bear that left them. The width of the front feet and the length of the hind feet are the important measurements to observe.

The width of a small cub's front foot is around three inches. This, of course, increases with age and physical growth. When sows reach maturity, the width of their front feet rarely exceeds six inches and the length of their hind feet ten or eleven inches. Mature males, however, may achieve a front paw width of eight inches and a hind foot length of sixteen inches. Anytime you observe a track this large, you know it was left by a huge male bear.

Wildlife and hunting guides on Kodiak Island have a rule of thumb by which they evaluate the physical size of a bear by measuring bear tracks. Some take the width of the front foot pad in inches, add one or two inches and multiply that number by one foot. Thus a bear that has left a track six

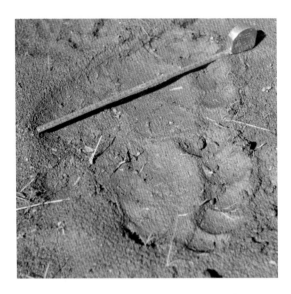

FIGURE 17 *A large male in Karluk Lake, Kodiak National Wildlife Refuge, left a footprint sixteen inches long and eight inches wide.*

inches wide is close to an eight-foot bear, and one that has left an eight-inch-wide track is approximately ten feet tall.

When a hunter has taken a bear, the size of the bear's hide can be measured when the fleshed-out hide is laid flat on the ground. Two measurements are added together: the length from the tip of the longest front claw on one side to the tip of the longest front claw on the opposite side, plus the length from the tip of the nose to the tail. That figure is then divided by two. A ten-foot hide is considered to be an impressively large bear. Sometimes, hunters stretch the hides in both directions to achieve greater dimensions, or find ways to skin a bear to increase the length of the hide. Because of the variability in hide measure-

ments, skull size is used instead to determine the official trophy size of bears. It is a more accurate method and leaves little room for cheating.

Great variations in the size and growth of young bears occur in family groups and even among littermates. Just as in a family of domestic pigs or dogs, an occasional runt is born. Genetic inheritance is also an influence. The offspring of a small sow and boar probably will not reach the enormous size of the offspring of a very large female and a huge male.

The ultimate growth bears achieve also depends upon the abundance and quality of available food. Bears inhabiting an area with a luxuriant supply of vegetation, berries, and fishery resources tend to become larger than those living in regions where food is scarce. That is one reason why coastal brown bears are physically larger than interior bears, which have fewer rich protein resources available.

Judging the size of a bear by sight is extremely difficult, and accuracy comes only with a lot of experience. This is especially true when the animal is alone. Quite a few times I have heard an inexperienced bear viewer remark about the huge size of a small two- or three-year-old bear. Then when a really large bear rises out of the grass and dwarfs the small animal, a viewer realizes his misjudgment.

If a bear is facing you, look at the width between the ears. In older bears, this space is much greater in relation to the rest of the head than in smaller and younger bears. Also look at the distance between the front legs, including the chest. Large bears look massive in a frontal view. Their legs are spread wide apart to support their hefty bulk. A deep-slung belly is indicative of a very large, adult bear.

Movements also give an indication of size and age. Animals that are running around and playing are usually young bears. Older, larger bears seem to walk in a slow, deliberate shuffle. Young animals move more rapidly and tend to change pace often.

Bears may continue to live many years after they have reached maturity. As in humans and other mammal species, lifespan varies immensely. Females tend to live longer than males. Perhaps part of this difference can be attributed to the fact that mature males fight more often and may suffer injuries that limit their ability to gather adequate food supplies.

One summer I watched a large boar with a deformed hip try unsuccessfully to catch salmon while other bears had no fishing problems. Time after time he limped to the middle of the stream and made short lunges, but his movements were too slow, resulting in failure. He appeared lean and had not accumulated needed fat reserves. I felt sorry for the old boar. It is doubtful that he survived the next hibernation period.

In hunted populations, hunters try for the larger trophy bears, reducing the chances of the males to survive very long. Suffice it to say, a bear that reaches the age of twenty years is an old bear. A few bears, however, have been documented to reach more than thirty years of age in the wild.

On August 7, 1959, I tagged a three-year-old female on Canyon Creek near Karluk Lake on Kodiak Island. We placed tags numbered 555 and 556 in the left and right ears. A hunter shot the sow thirty-two years later in the fall of 1991 within a few miles of where I originally tagged her. She still retained tag #555. The old sow, therefore, was thirty-five years old and is, to my knowledge, the oldest bear ever recorded in the wild. That is what I call an old, old bear.

FIGURE 18   *These two large males are fighting over the right to a favorite fishing spot below Brooks Falls, Katmai National Park.*

4

IN BEAR SOCIETY

LOW CLOUDS SLID ACROSS THE SKIES, ENGULFING *mountaintops and filling the alpine valleys with fog. A steady drizzle of rain obscured Connecticut Creek, which wound a snakelike course through this part of Kodiak Island. A sow, with two small cubs trailing, emerged out of the mists and followed a ridge that led down toward the creek.*

The mother appeared nervous as she approached the stream, checking often to make sure that her cubs were not far behind. On a bank high above the creek she stopped, rose on her hind legs, and sniffed the air. The female recognized the scent of a three-year-old bear that she had met, challenged, and chased the day before. It was fishing downstream around the first bend. She dropped to all fours, and then moved to the edge of the bank, facing upstream and staring intently, as droplets of rain dripped from her long guard hairs. One of her cubs also stood on its hind feet to look, bracing one forefoot on her side to maintain its balance.

Detecting nothing more, the family followed a muddy trail down a steep bank to the edge of the creek and stood, carefully scrutinizing it in both directions. An abundance of red salmon splashed and moved about the shallow water. Some were in the process of spawning, while others were fighting their way farther upstream.

Not seeing or smelling any other bears, the sow parked her cubs on the stream bank and waded into the water. Immediately, red salmon skittered through the shallows, triggering a chase. She galloped downstream and became engulfed in the flying spray of white foamy water. One salmon made a wrong turn and shot up on a gravel bar, fully exposed. The bear quickly pinned the fish with her claws, firmly clenched it in her teeth, and waded back upstream toward the cubs.

On the bank, the mother tore pieces of flesh from the salmon and gulped down a mouthful. Between bites she raised her head and scanned the horizon for any intruders. The cubs squalled constantly, pleading for a bite of salmon, but the sow was hungry and ignored them. She greedily consumed the entire fish in about five gulps. A few tidbits remained on the ground, which the mother left for the cubs, and again she entered the creek.

This time the sow moved upstream, chasing several salmon without success.

She was engrossed in her fishing when a large, young male bear came around a bend of the stream. The mother stopped and, after a quick look, launched herself like a projectile toward the intruding bear. He debated for a moment whether to fight or flee, for he was larger and outweighed the sow by 150 pounds. She wanted this fishing hole for herself, and also feared for her cubs, who were sitting on the bank in wide-eyed terror.

The female slammed into the young boar as he started to turn. Her hurtling momentum knocked him off his feet. She lunged for his neck, but missed and sank her teeth into his shoulders instead. The battle raged as he bit back, burying his teeth into her leg. Somehow in all the roaring fury and splashing of water, he regained his footing, turned, and ran for his life. She chased him for another hundred feet, and then stopped.

She chomped her teeth several times and ran back to her cubs. The excited sow stood for many minutes, nervously huffing and looking upstream to make sure her adversary did not return. Satisfied that the young male had left the creek, she resumed fishing.

In general, brown bears are solitary animals. They wander through the remote regions of their home range, having little contact with one another. The exceptions to this lonely life are family relationships—cubs still dependent on their mother for food and protection, young siblings that remain together for a year or two after being evicted by their mother, and males and females that form pairs during the breeding season. Bears will also congregate at a concentrated food source.

A mother with young cubs has an immense responsibility, and most females take this duty very seriously. They become wary and protective of their offspring and often seek remote areas far removed from other bears. They watch their cubs closely, and if the youngsters stray too far from their mother, they are quickly brought back by vocal commands or a physical reprimand. The latter may be in the form of a nudge or a quick cuff with a paw. As the cubs get older and more independent, sows tend to let them stray further.

A mother's most difficult period is during salmon season, when she has to leave the cubs for short periods while fishing. In some instances, she may stray quite far before she makes a catch. Often during these short separations the cubs become nervous. In a prolonged absence, the youngsters may become alarmed and leave their assigned area. This can lead to all kinds of stressful experiences for the cubs and the mother. If they are not present when she returns, the sow immediately starts a search and attempts to follow their scent trails to locate them.

Cubs left unattended sometimes become endangered if they stray too far or come in contact with other bears. In July 1995, several photographers and I were watching a sow with a single cub we called Tiny. The mother and cub were sitting on a riverbank when the sow spotted a salmon splashing in the river about forty yards away. In a flash, the sow plunged down the bank and into the water, chasing the salmon around a curve. She caught the salmon, but instead of returning to the cub, she stopped on a nearby gravel bar to eat it.

Tiny became agitated when its mother did not return and started running along the bank. When it failed to find her, the cub headed across a huge flat meadow. We were dismayed as we watched it run toward an ocean beach. It disappeared over a rise a half mile away. At this point I said to my guests, "Let's get out of here. I don't want to be blamed for the missing cub." We withdrew up the river another 150 yards.

After a while the mother returned and, as expected, was distraught when she failed to find her cub. She circled the immediate vicinity, searching desperately. When she picked up the cub's scent trail, she loped across the meadow in hot pursuit. She was excited and her constant growling and huffing indicated anger. She too disappeared over the rise near the beach. About the same time, Tiny reemerged further down the ridge, heading back in our direction. As the cub came running and squalling, my photographer friends and I quickly crossed the river and got on a high knoll where we could watch the outcome. We did not want to be in the path of the sow if she failed to find her cub.

Tiny arrived back at the original site and began to run in circles. The sow returned over the ridge on Tiny's trail, still loping and emitting growls of alarm. Several bears in the area saw her coming and ran to get out of her way. Tiny made several false starts to leave, but before the cub wandered far, the mother got close enough to spot it. They had a joyful reunion; needless to say, we also were very happy.

After observing such a situation, you can easily understand how cubs can get separated from their mothers and, under the right circumstances, be killed or injured by another bear that did not like the intrusion. Both Larry Aumiller and Thomas Bledsoe reported witnessing such a situation at

McNeil River. Families fishing in close proximity often left their cubs at the same site or very near to one another. Sometimes the cubs intermingled. On several occasions the men observed a sow returning, and then departing with more cubs than she had brought. In other instances both sows returned at the same time and, in the melee, departed with the wrong cubs. This "cub swapping" was usually temporary, but a few times the new mother permanently adopted the wrong cubs. I have never observed cub swapping and believe it would occur only in closely grouped bears, such as at McNeil where a number of families fish near one another.

When left by themselves in such concentrations, cubs occasionally get in the path of a belligerent bear. This can lead to severe injury or even death if the sow is not there to defend it.

The mother generally weans cubs in the third spring when they are a little over two years old. It must be a traumatic experience for the juvenile bears to be evicted by a mother who has fed and protected them all their lives. They often try to follow their mother for several days after being rejected, but she continues to harass them away from her. Gradually the young bears realize they must fend for themselves.

Siblings in a litter commonly remain together the first summer after weaning, and sometimes for two years. Gradually the bonds weaken and they spend more time separated. Eventually they join the single bear world.

The social life of adult breeding pairs is of much shorter duration. Males seek out females and the pair may remain together for a few days to two weeks. Their social interaction during the breeding season is described in chapter 5.

In addition to these three family situations, bears are often forced into contact with each other when they compete for food resources. The most pronounced example of this occurs during the salmon-spawning season in Alaska's coastal streams and rivers. Competition for the fish is intense; bears using any given area form a pecking order in which individual bears become dominant over others. Eventually each animal learns its status within that particular group or society of bears.

Large adult males are usually at the top of the hierarchy, followed by sows with cubs. Next come single adult sows, young males, then young females, and last the smaller juveniles. But bears, like people, have different temperaments, creating exceptions to this generalized social order. Some are extremely belligerent and seem to walk around with chips on their shoulders, ready to fight any other bear that gets in their way. Others are docile or shy and try to avoid fights, even though they may be physically larger and stronger. Fights, threats, bluffs, various body postures, growls, and other signals maintain this social order, which is recognized in the bear world. An individual's status may change. When older animals lose some of their physical abilities, due to old age or injuries, they may drop down the social ladder. Young bears move up as they grow and become physically stronger and braver.

Sows with cubs often become highly stressed when they are forced into contact with other bears and at times they act irrationally. They can become agitated and challenge huge boars that come too close to their cubs. Thus, they often become dominant over males that are far larger than they are. However, after they wean their cubs, their aggression may diminish, possibly resulting in a drop in social status.

Most brown bears in Alaska are not subjected to these very intense, crowded situations because the majority of bears feed in long, meandering salmon

FIGURE 19   *A small cub is climbing up for a piggy-back ride in Hallo Bay, Katmai National Park.*

streams where they tend to disperse, avoiding close, competitive contact. Some wary bears will steer clear of crowded salmon streams all summer and remain in more remote regions feeding on sedges, berries, and other vegetation. Other bears fish at night to avoid the crowds. Just like humans, some thrive on close social contact and others sacrifice to live a lonely life.

In places where bears are thrust closely together, they each have their individual space or distance at which they will either fight or flee. One summer I guided a small group of people photographing a sow with a single cub. Over a period of several days she became unperturbed by our presence and let us work close by without showing any signs of aggression. Then one day as we were photographing her, a young male approached from behind us. The sow became increasingly agitated as the male grazed nearer. She constantly raised her head, watching his progress. Finally when he came within sixty yards, she suddenly charged straight toward him, rushing past us not fifty feet away. The young bear saw her coming, turned tail, and ran. After a brief chase the sow returned to her cub, sauntering past us, oblivious to our presence. It was apparent that she was less concerned about us than about the young male.

Bears do learn to avoid certain individuals and to tolerate others. Their actions probably relate to experience. They may have been harassed or threatened by one particular animal and learned that others are amiable toward them. Some individuals even become friends and play together for short periods or feed and rest near one another. They seem to have both enemies and friends.

It is unusual for bears to feed on salmon together in dense concentrations as they do at McNeil Falls and Brooks Falls on the Alaska Peninsula. In these unique situations, land and water features are natural barriers that cause the salmon to concentrate. Biologists have reported seeing more than sixty brown bears at McNeil River Falls at one time. Standing on a small knoll overlooking the Katmai Coast, I have counted over thirty bears in the nearby sedge meadows. Along the O'Malley River on Kodiak Island I have identified up to fifty brown bears feeding in an area of only one square mile during the salmon spawning season. Because most people visit these unusually crowded sites to view bears, they often get the idea that bears are always social and come together to feed. But this is not true most of the year. As soon as the food source disappears, bears are quick to spread out, so confrontations are fewer and hierarchy is less obvious.

In 1996 I observed the arrival of the first salmon at Hallo Creek. Six to eight bears stood in the tidal surf waiting for salmon to leave the ocean waters and start up the shallow stream. They were all competing for the same few salmon and sometimes two bears chased the same fish. This resulted in a few mild squabbles, the bigger bear usually winning the skirmish. Finally, two adult boars almost collided, greatly annoying the larger boar who charged his competitor. They slammed into each other with considerable impact and the fight began. Amidst much roaring, biting, and clawing, the smaller animal finished on the bottom, struggling for his life. When he finally extracted himself from under the large boar, he managed to escape. I could see that the loser had been severely bitten several times; despite his thick coat of hair, blood streamed down his leg and side. He left the fishing to the winner, limping back to the sedge flats still hungry.

Old males usually have numerous scars on their bodies as a result of such encounters. During the breeding season, mature males often fight desperately to gain the possession of a female. Sometimes these battles occur on precipitous mountain slopes, resulting in one or both falling down steep cliffs and becoming badly injured. Several years ago we found the carcass of a boar at the bottom of a high rock cliff along the Katmai Coast. An autopsy revealed that this bear had received fatal internal injuries from a fall. We speculated that he had fallen over the cliff during a mating fight.

During the breeding season, males do pursue sows with cubs. A number of people have witnessed boars killing cubs under such circumstances. A sow will aggressively defend her cubs, but when she has two or more, the pursuing boar is often able to separate one from the group and kill it. This is particularly true in rough mountainous terrain where very young cubs may have difficulty keeping up with their mothers.

I have never witnessed such a kill, but on Kodiak Island we examined the stomach contents of two large males taken by hunters. They revealed the remains of small cubs. On another occasion I found a dead cub on a high snowfield on Kodiak Island. The tracks in the snow indicated that a fight had taken place between a boar and a sow with small cubs, and that one of the cubs had become a victim. Daniel Zatz, a cinematographer in Homer, Alaska, actually photographed the killing of a cub by an adult male at McNeil Falls. Larry Aumiller also documented several observations of cubs being killed at McNeil River; adult females, however, were the culprits just as often as were adult males.

A lot of strife exists among bears; fights sometimes end in death, even among juvenile and

FIGURE 20   *This old male at Hallo Bay, Katmai National Park, has numerous shoulder wounds. He probably lost a fight with a younger male.*

mature animals. Once while conducting research on Kodiak Island, my assistants and I found two bears killed and partially eaten by others. They had been caught in foot snares, and thus were handicapped in defending themselves. We returned to one of the kill sites several times over the next few days, and each time it was evident that additional flesh had been eaten, until one day only the skeleton remained. Surrounding tracks indicated that the bear was eaten by a sow with a yearling cub.

The social life of brown bears is an intriguing aspect of the bear's world. Though solitary much of their lives, they readily adapt when forced together. The group develops rules that most bears learn to follow. As in human society, young bears are protected and nurtured by their mothers. As they grow and become teenagers, they are given more freedom and responsibility until, finally, they mature and find their own place in the pecking order of bear society.

FIGURE 21   *Brown bears mate in the spring. They are polygamous: one male often breeds with several females.*

5

THE MATING GAME

SPLIT-EAR, THE DARK EIGHT-YEAR-OLD BOAR, HAD *been grazing peacefully on Dumpling Mountain near Brooks Lake since he emerged from hibernation in late April. The abundance of succulent sedges, grasses, and angelica shoots had kept him content to remain on the south-facing slope. He enjoyed a solitary life and purposely evaded other bears that he occasionally scented or sighted in the distance.*

Toward the end of May he got an impulse to travel. He moved across the top of Dumpling Mountain and began to descend its north slope toward Naknek Lake. About halfway down, the wandering male crossed the path of an adult sow and followed her trail.

Split-Ear became extremely excited when he sniffed a patch of grass where the sow had urinated, for his keen nose detected that she was approaching her estrus period. The big boar now had an urge to mate. He followed the trail at a rapid rate and ignored some of the choice salad shoots covering that part of the mountain; food was not on his mind. The sow had stopped to rest, so the eager male soon caught up with her. She spotted him and sat up to watch his movements. Split-Ear cautiously circled the cream-colored sow, but carefully avoided any aggressive moves that might frighten this lovely female. She was a little alarmed by the huge, bulky boar, but she did not discourage his advances. When they were less than twenty feet apart, they sat and stared at each other. Split-Ear coyly began to graze on some nearby sedges, occasionally sneaking a glance at the sow. She continued to watch him and seemed fascinated by his movements. Gradually he grazed toward her, and eventually the pair stood nose to nose, smelling one another. He sniffed her entire body, moving his nose down her back, under her belly, and finally to her genital area. She was coming into estrus but was not quite ready to mate. They began to cuff each other playfully with their paws. The suitor rubbed against the sow's body, but when he clumsily flung one front leg across her back, she moved away.

The courtship continued for two days. Split-Ear constantly fed near the blond sow and occasionally tried to mount her, but she continued to deny his advances. On the third day and after many attempts, she stood still when he climbed aboard. He remained on the sow for forty-five minutes, intermit-

tently making deep pelvic thrusts and then resting. The coupling continued off and on all afternoon. When she finally lay down to rest, he snuggled beside her.

On the fifth day, as they were grazing a few feet apart, Split-Ear's keen nostrils caught the scent of another bear. He rose to his hind legs and sniffed the air currents, looking nervously in the direction of the scent. It was a strong odor and Split-Ear knew another boar was near. He became agitated and popped his jaws several times, foaming saliva oozing from his lips. He moved a short distance and climbed up onto a small knoll. The strong scent and cracking brush told him the other male was coming rapidly. The newcomer had also smelled the sow in estrus. As Split-Ear watched and issued warnings by stomping his feet, a huge dark boar stepped out of the brush. The two adversaries were of nearly equal size and weight. The newcomer also had an old scar across his shoulder blade and numerous cuts on his face, attesting to many previous battles.

Split-Ear made a few threatening moves, but the intruding boar held his ground. This male was obviously going to contest Split-Ear for the female. They circled each other at a distance for a few minutes, and then Split-Ear charged. His body hurtled toward the newcomer with all the fury that he could muster and he slammed into his foe. The slope was steep and the impact sent them rolling down the mountain in a blur of flying claws and flashing teeth. Biting and roaring, the bears fought viciously. For a moment Split-Ear got a good hold on the stranger's neck. His powerful jaws bit deep and blood oozed across the brown fur. The newcomer, however, broke loose and ripped a piece of flesh and hide from Split-Ear's shoulder.

The female watched the battle and nervously chewed on a few shoots of fresh cow parsnip. This was no mere squabble, but a fight to the finish and each contender knew his life hung in the balance. As roars rent the air and hair flew, the newcomer got a stranglehold on Split-Ear's neck and held him to the ground. Split-Ear tried to break free, but couldn't; he knew he was outmatched. He finally tore loose, jumped to his feet, and fled down the mountain, leaving the victor with the prize. He was in a bad mood and highly stressed as he stumbled down the slope with new neck wounds and a badly torn shoulder. His left ear now flopped loosely on his head and blood streamed down his face.

To the winner go the spoils and the newcomer moved toward the sow. She accepted his advances and they remained together for a week, coupling often, just as she and Split-Ear had done in their brief courtship. Split-Ear, however, moaned and grumbled constantly as he moved across the valley toward Mount Kelez. Another two weeks passed before his wounds began to heal and he could find another female that was ready to pursue the mating game.

Bears having sex are comical to watch. Males may try all kinds of antics to bring females into the breeding mood. They are often mismatched in physical proportions, and when a boar's full weight comes down on a sow, she may be squashed to the ground.

The first time I observed a breeding pair was on a July evening at Karluk Lake. A friend and I were traveling across the lake in a skiff and observed the bears along the shoreline. We cut the motor and rowed silently toward them. As we drew closer, I saw that they were coupled, but the female became nervous at our presence and broke free of the boar. He tried to mount her again, completely oblivious of us, but she thwarted his advances by simply sitting down on her rear end in shallow water. He straddled his mate and attempted to lift her body up with his forelegs, but she consistently managed to sit back down. The boar then got in front of the sow, and from a distance of ten feet deliberately splashed water in her face with his forepaws. He continued these antics for fifteen minutes, but to no avail; she kept her rear end submerged. She was obviously going to refuse his advances in our presence. We discreetly rowed around a point and out of sight. I stepped ashore and peeked over an alder bush with my binoculars. From there I spotted them on the shoreline, coupled. Apparently she desired privacy.

Another summer I was on the Alaska Peninsula with photographer friends, and over the course of several days we followed a breeding pair. The large male was persistent in pursuing the female and he constantly approached her. He attempted to mount the sow, but each time she resisted his advances. Two other boars also tried to woo the female, but her lover, who seemed to be dominant, always chased them away. With several boars trying to approach her, we were sure she was in estrus, but the sow continued to reject the advances of any of the males. We watched the one-sided romance for two days. The large boar constantly followed the female, occasionally grazing, and made several more approaches, but each time she prevented his efforts. They even slept side by side, but no sex occurred. Then on the evening of the second day, as the sun sank behind the mountains and the soft evening light illuminated the grassy meadow, he tried again. This time she accepted him and they coupled. He remained on top of her for thirty-five minutes, their entwined bodies silhouetted in the late evening light. It was a very romantic setting and we humorously speculated that perhaps she waited for that special sentimental evening to consummate sex. Perhaps our speculation bore some truth, for the next day the couple repeated the courtship. The boar again attempted to mount the sow on numerous occasions during the long daylight hours, but each time she moved away. Then as the sun disappeared and an evening mist descended on the meadow, she once again accepted him. In the gathering darkness they locked in breeding position.

Of such is bear romance!

The brown bear breeding season lasts from mid-May to mid-July, but mating activity is at its peak during the month of June. Mature males travel extensively in search of females in heat. Once together, the boar and the sow form pair bonds that last from a day to several weeks. They remain near each other while feeding, sleeping, or resting. They are both coy in their courtship display, often rubbing together or gently cuffing one another in apparent foreplay. A male may follow a female around for several days, however, and attempt to breed a number of times before she finally becomes receptive and lets him consummate the courtship. It is an act that they both seem to enjoy. He mounts her from the rear and wraps his huge forelegs around her body. Once penetration with the penis is achieved, he initiates deep pelvic thrusts. The breeding act is not a hurried affair and often lasts for forty-five minutes or more, as the male alternately thrusts and rests, sometimes falling asleep during the process.

Female brown bears often mate with several boars during the course of a week or two. Males may also mate with more than one sow. The females do not all come into estrus at the same time, so the boars have one to two months to look for sows that are in the mating mood.

Males will sometimes fight furiously to gain the "rights" to a female, especially if the two males are of equal physical size and temperament. At other times a small male will simply leave the female when a large boar approaches. Most older boars have numerous scars on their bodies from such encounters. The female takes a passive attitude in such disputes and simply remains in the area to see who her next suitor will be.

Males have a large baculum (penis bone), which helps them enter the female during the breeding act. The baculum ossifies at about two years of age and this long, slightly curved bone increases in weight and length with age until maturity. The penis bone in a young bear may be only two inches long, while the baculum of an adult male is from six to eight inches in length.

If breeding is successful and the female egg or eggs are fertilized with the male sperm, they go through an unusual physiological stage, called delayed implantation. The fertilized egg briefly undergoes cell division, but instead of the reproductive process continuing until the fetus is formed, the tiny blastocyst does not yet implant on the uterine wall, temporarily halting development. Instead it floats freely in her reproductive

FIGURE 22   *A yearling cub at Hallo Bay, Katmai National Park, nurses its reclining mother.*

tract for the next four to six months. About the time the female enters hibernation, the blastocyst implants on the uterus wall and begins to develop once again. Delayed implantation is the reason young cubs born in the den in January or February are extremely small, naked, and relatively helpless, weighing about one pound. They crawl across the mother's hair, attach to a teat, and begin suckling the warm, rich milk. While in the den, the mother has to convert her fat reserves into milk to nurse the cubs, since she does not eat during this period.

Sows may have from one to four cubs, and most commonly have two or three. To accommodate and feed them, females have six mammary glands, or teats. Four of these are located on the chest just behind the front legs and two are between the hind legs. It is difficult to know what body position the sow takes while nursing her cubs in the den, but once they are out in the open, the mother usually lies on her back in a reclining position, preferably leaning against a knoll or ridge so she can quickly lift her head. As the cubs crawl up on her chest and grab a teat, she often uses her front feet to cradle them to her breast. A sow is particularly nervous while nursing the cubs and apparently feels vulnerable on her back. She constantly raises her head to look around, especially if other bears are in the vicinity. If another bear approaches too closely, she immediately jumps up, ending the feeding.

The cubs make an audible purring sound while nursing, similar to the purring of a cat. Apparently it is a way of showing contentment. They usually suckle for five to ten minutes and change teats quite frequently, seemingly favoring the upper four chest teats over the lower two. I have rarely seen cubs nurse while the sow is standing, although they do try. They let their mother know of their hunger by begging. Squalling loudly, they follow her at

FIGURE 23   *Females have six mammary glands; four are located behind the front legs and two are near the rear legs. Note also the characteristic white collar of this cub in Hallo Bay, Katmai National Park.*

close quarters and sometimes seize a teat for a few moments, but she usually walks away.

One summer I watched a sow with a single cub far out on the low tidal flats in Hallo Bay. She was digging clams and really did not want to take time to suckle the cub, who became persistent with its begging, bawling louder and louder. She continued to dig clams and ignore the noisy pleading. She even left some clam tidbits for the cub, but apparently this did not satisfy its hunger for long. It stopped to gulp the clam, and then started whining again. The cub seemed literally to be screaming, "Please, momma, I'm hungry!" But she paid no heed. The cub then took on a more desperate, staccato barking, similar to the noise a cub makes when in extreme distress or when lost. Still she would not let it nurse. Finally she left the flats and walked to a sloping gravel beach, turned over, and let the cub have its meal.

Some mothers get irritated at cubs that constantly bawl and beg for milk and will turn around and cuff the offspring with a paw or nip them with teeth. Usually, though, they simply ignore the begging cubs until they are ready, and then find a suitable spot to nurse the young. Cubs continue to nurse through the second summer, but as they grow older and partake of more solid food, the nursing becomes less frequent.

The number of cubs a sow produces in her lifetime depends on when she reaches sexual maturity, the frequency and size of litters, her success in raising the cubs to weaning age, and the age at which she dies or ceases to produce cubs. My studies on Kodiak Island indicate that most females reach sexual maturity and begin to breed when they are four to six years old. Under ideal conditions a sow first breeds at four or five years, has a litter of two or three cubs, weans them when they are two years old, then immediately breeds again and has cubs the following spring. A sow could successfully raise a litter of cubs every third year until she is at least twenty years old. A few female brown bears produce cubs beyond twenty years of age. Larry Aumiller and Dick Sellers reported that one sow at McNeil River had a single cub at the age of twenty-six!

Theoretically, each sow in a population is thus capable of having at least five litters in her lifetime and adding ten to fifteen cubs to the population— but this scenario is very unlikely. Studies have indicated that cub death during the first year of life is significant, and may be in excess of 30 percent in some regions. Some sows lose one or two cubs in a litter, whereas others lose their entire litter. In some areas many females do not produce a successful litter until they are seven or eight years of age, and some sows nurse cubs for as long as three years. Under these conditions they would have a litter only every fourth year.

A sow suckling her cubs or a pair of adults breeding are intimate acts in a bear's life that are rarely observed by people. Of course, viewers should take care never to approach a mating pair too closely; males are often very aggressive in defending their mates. Perhaps one of the best places to witness these behaviors is in the numerous sedge meadows along the Alaska Peninsula. Bears congregate to feed on the plants in June and early July, with June being the peak of the breeding season. The terrain is flat and unobstructed by tall vegetation. If one watches a group of bears long enough, the chances of observing a breeding pair are quite good. Watch even longer and a sow with cubs will eventually stop grazing, turn over, and let her cubs suckle. The opportunity to observe either of these activities is always the highlight of a bear-viewing experience, witnessed by only the few willing to venture onto the bears' own turf.

FIGURE 24   *Trails like this one in Hallo Bay, Katmai National Park, crisscross bear country.*

6

TRAVELS AND TRAILS

THE OLD FEMALE BEAR LIFTED HER HEAD SEVERAL *times, then sluggishly laid it down and slept again. Fifteen minutes later she awoke and sat up on her haunches. She was still groggy, but gradually she focused on the surroundings. Her three yearling cubs lay nearby, sound asleep. Everything was strange and unfamiliar. Mountains were everywhere—mountains she did not recognize. Saltwater lapped at the nearby beach and several harbor seals frolicked in the surf. The new sights and smells confounded the old female. She could not know that a park ranger had deemed her and the cubs a menace to campers at the Brooks Lake campground and decided to move the family across the mountains to Kukak Bay.*

FIGURE 25   *Brown bears are excellent swimmers, though river crossings may be perilous, particularly for young cubs.*

As she sat, trying to focus on her surroundings, the three cubs gradually awoke, stood up, and shook themselves. The family continued to sleep on and off all afternoon, but became more and more alert. Momma, as she was dubbed by park personnel, began to feed on some saltwater sedge. She had never tasted this plant before, but it was delicious and the whole family began to fill their stomachs with the succulent green food.

For days they wandered around the Kukak flats and grazed on the abundant sedges. They also checked the streams in the bay for salmon, but none were present as they had been in the Brooks River. The old female was bewildered and edgy in this unfamiliar environment. She longed to be back home at Brooks, but where was home?

With something inside her brain directing her, she led her family along a southwesterly journey, along the shorelines and occasionally across small peninsulas of land. They often followed old bear trails. Several times Momma smelled the presence of other bears, but being in unfamiliar country and among strangers, she avoided confrontations with them whenever possible.

At the head of Dakavak Bay, on the twelfth day of their trip, Momma sniffed the scent of meat. She wasn't sure what kind of animal it might be, but the strong smell had the whole family galloping toward the food source. Their keen noses directed them to a dead sea lion that had been deposited on the gravel beach by a recent high tide. As they approached, a red fox scurried from the carcass and several gulls took to the skies. The big sea lion had been dead only a few days. Extremely hungry, they alternately gorged and slept by the carcass. Another small bear approached in the late afternoon and Momma raced toward it. Her cubs followed. She was willing to fight for this food source, but did not need to. The stranger realized it was outnumbered and fled from the scene.

By the next morning only the hide and the skeleton remained. With full stomachs the family continued its journey, arriving in Katmai Bay on the sixteenth day. Here they stayed for several days, feeding on vegetation and a few berries. Momma spotted a young seal pup that had crawled out on a sandy knoll. The tide had retreated and left it far from the sea. She had no trouble in cutting off its retreat. She killed the pup with a quick bite of her powerful jaws and the family had another meat dinner.

The bears were now southeast of Brooks Lake and the urge to move north was compelling. They headed across the sandy, volcanic flats, shuffling steadily toward the mountains. Numerous channels of the Katmai River confronted them. The bears waded across some with ease; other times they were forced to swim. The main channel was swift and swollen from several days of rain, but Momma did not hesitate, plunging in and swimming strongly. She was gradually swept downriver. Her three cubs followed, but they had a more difficult time. One cub was a weak swimmer; the current swept it around a swift curve of the river and pulled it under a logjam. The cub never surfaced.

Momma was distraught and ran up and down the riverbank searching for her cub, but toward evening she gave up the effort. The remaining family members continued across the alluvial plain and late that night reached higher ground. They scooped out depressions and rested throughout the night.

The next morning, they climbed higher into the mountains, following Mageik Creek until they reached Katmai Pass. The last few days had been tough traveling, and now they faced the Valley of Ten Thousand Smokes. It is a valley with sparse vegetation, but Momma was now driven with a sense that she was near home territory. She allowed a little rest, and then led the march across the desolate landscape. On the twenty-second day a park ranger spotted them at Three Forks and reported the sighting to the chief ranger, who was not happy with the news.

Here the bears found fresh green vegetation and stopped to fill their hungry stomachs since they had not eaten for four days. They continued to feed, travel, and rest as they descended the mountain slopes toward the Brooks River. On the twenty-seventh day they arrived back at Brooks Camp. A sense of peace came over the old sow as she felt at home again, even though she had lost one of her cubs. The chief ranger, however, was alarmed and put a notice on the bulletin board for all rangers to keep an eye on Momma and her mischievous cubs.

———————

The homing instinct of brown bears is quite strong. Many seem to have an uncanny ability to find their way home even when transported across high mountains and other barriers. Momma was moved sixty air miles from her habitual use area around Brooks River and had to cross some formidable obstacles, but she returned in twenty-seven days. One might speculate that her three yearling cubs slowed her speed of return.

The ability of brown bears to return to their home site after being transplanted varies with individual bears, just as it does with other animals such as domestic dogs. Some seem to have a compass in their heads. In general, however, the greater the distance bears are moved, the less likely they are to return.

In the Susitna River drainage of southcentral Alaska, biologists Sterling Miller and Warren Ballard captured and transplanted forty-seven brown bears in 1979 in an experiment to reduce moose-calf predation. Adequate movement data were obtained on twenty adults to evaluate their homing ability. They were released an average distance of 123 miles from their capture site, and 60 percent returned to their point of capture in an average of 58 days. The longest return movement was 160 miles. Of nine cubs and yearlings transplanted with their mothers, only three survived the ordeal.

Lee Glenn and Lee Miller reported moving a three-year-old female brown bear from Chignik Lagoon across the Aleutian Range to Black Lake, an airline distance of twenty-six miles. She returned to her capture site within twenty-four hours! Another epic journey by a transplanted brown bear was reported by Julius Reynolds. A three-year-old male was transported from Cordova, Alaska, to Montague Island in Prince William Sound. It returned in twenty-eight days. In order to accomplish this, the bear had to swim across a body of water with strong tidal currents for a minimum distance of six miles.

Of course, these examples of bear movements were induced by man and did not occur as a result of natural bear travels.

Without human interference, the geographic region a bear inhabits during the course of an entire year is referred to as its home range. Unlike many animals that defend their territories against other individuals of the same species, brown bears have overlapping home ranges that they often share with other bears for various periods of time. The size of these areas varies considerably, and is influenced by the age and sex of the individual animals, availability of food resources, denning sites, cover, and various barriers, such as large lakes that affect the bears' movements.

Brown bears tend to have smaller home ranges in geographic regions where plenty of food, denning sites, and cover are available within a confined area. On the Alaska Peninsula many bears den in the mountains and, after emerging from hibernation in the spring, travel across the coastal plains to the seacoast, a distance of twenty to fifty miles, to search for marine mammals, an early spring food source. In contrast, some bears around Karluk Lake on Kodiak Island den and feed all year in the same drainage, requiring very small seasonal movements.

Females tend to have smaller home ranges than adult males. As an example, Momma normally spent the spring near Brooks Camp grazing on vegetation until the salmon arrived in the Brooks River around the first of July. She fished the river from July through October; occasionally, however, she and her cubs moved to Margot Creek, a distance of five or six miles, and remained in this drainage for a week or two during the peak of the salmon run. Then they returned to Brooks. She denned on Mount Kelez, five miles south of

Brooks. Her annual use area was confined to a relatively small region of only a few square miles.

One adult male, whom I tracked with a radio collar at Brooks in the fall, remained in this vicinity until October 19. He then traveled to Margot Creek and continued up the Savonoski River until he reached the Rainbow River on October 29, approximately thirty-six miles from Brooks. There he fed on a late run of salmon through mid-November and apparently denned in this area. In the spring he moved northwest to King Salmon Creek, sixty-four miles from his denning site, and was shot by a hunter outside the park. His travels were much greater than Momma's.

In some areas, such as southwest Kodiak Island, bears travel extensively between various drainages and their movements are timed to coincide with the salmon runs that peak at different periods in different streams and rivers. Apparently many of their travel and feeding patterns are traditional habits established by several generations of female bears. The cubs learn the sites and timing of the salmon runs from their mothers, and in turn pass the information on to their offspring. Knowledge of other food sources is also transmitted in this way, as explained in chapter 7.

The geographic features of a region dictate movements to a great extent. Large bodies of water or steep mountain ranges tend to divert bear movements, whereas low mountain passes become corridors for bears to travel from one valley to another. Networks of trails link various feeding areas and drainages. From the air these pronounced bear roads look like interconnecting highways.

Many major routes have been traveled for centuries and in places are worn several feet deep. In alpine areas, where soil is firm or gravelly, the footpaths often take the form of spaced depressions as

FIGURE 26   *A sow and cub resting.*

bears have stepped precisely in one another's tracks for hundreds of years.

In wet muskeg areas, where tall vegetation is sparse, bear paths may be several feet wide. In following such routes myself I have often found two-lane trails. I am not sure whether the double lanes are caused by numerous bears being forced to pass each other or not. I suspect some bears may prefer a slightly different path, and eventually both lanes became established routes. In bear country, it behooves hikers to learn the location of the bear trails. They are usually the best paths to follow when traveling through wild country; in much of coastal Alaska, no man-made trails are present.

When cubs are with their mother, they of course follow and use her seasonal ranges. Once they are weaned and independent, they wander and eventually develop their own geographic region of travel. Female offspring tend to remain close to their

FIGURE 27 *Some bears are capable of running thirty-five miles per hour.*

mother's home range; young males wander widely in search of new feeding and denning areas.

Momma's two male cubs moved completely outside of Katmai National Park once they were weaned. Both were subsequently shot in the King Salmon area, approximately thirty-two miles from the Brooks River area they frequented with their mother. Apparently they were searching for a new home range when they met their ill fate.

Bears are more active during the early morning and late evening hours than they are during the middle of the day. I once recorded the intensity of bears' fishing efforts from dawn till dusk (4 AM to 10 PM) on Kodiak Island over a nine-day period in July. Very few bears were present at dawn, but soon thereafter they emerged from their beds and started to fish. The peak morning fishing effort occurred between 5 AM and 8 AM, and then dropped off drastically. After filling their stomachs with salmon, most of the bears rested through the midday period, although some bears always fished during the middle of the day. They again fished in great numbers in the evening hours between 6 PM and 10 PM. I was unable to conduct counts after dark, but judging from the sounds I heard, some bears continued to fish well into the night. Almost twice as many bears fished in the evening as in the morning.

Bears do travel and feed throughout the day, but the best time to see them in large numbers is in the morning and evening. Of course, other factors may affect bear activity, such as weather, tides, and various human disturbances. Low-flying airplanes and noisy helicopters may cause bears to leave favorite feeding sites for a time.

The speed at which bears usually travel can be deceiving. I have often watched large adult animals amble along a trail in an apparently slow shuffle. In reality, however, they can cross a valley or mountaintop quite rapidly with that methodical gait. On several occasions I have hiked parallel to bears as they followed a trail through a valley and I have almost had to run to keep up with their shuffling pace. Perhaps it is the appearance of a large animal taking those deliberate steps that is very misleading.

Bears are fast sprinters. With a sudden burst of speed they can capture a moose or caribou; however, they are no match for healthy animals over long distances out in the open. I once clocked a bear running down a gravel road in the Bells Flat area near Kodiak. The brown bear was of medium size and started running ahead of my car. I stepped on the gas to push the bear a little, and for several hundred yards the bear galloped along at a steady thirty-five miles per hour before it finally turned and ran off the road.

In the summer of 1997 I had the opportunity to measure the running speed of another young brown bear on the Kenai Peninsula. A friend and I had just loaded our canoe on our truck and headed down Swan Lake Road when a young bear appeared in front of us. I pushed the juvenile bear for about a quarter of a mile, but for all of its galloping effort, it never exceeded twenty miles per hour.

Suffice it to say, I would never try to outrun a brown bear.

I have always been astounded at the maze of trails that blanket good brown bear habitat. The trails wind across mountains and in and out of meadows, streams, and valleys. Their pattern is not apparent to us, but bears negotiate extremely complex trail networks to reach specific seasonal feeding and denning sites without a clock, calendar, or map. The inner compass that orients bears through vast wild lands remains an intriguing mystery.

FIGURE 28   *This group of bears is feeding on a whale that washed ashore on Hallo Bay on the Katmai Coast. Brown bears are usually solitary feeders, but may become more gregarious near an abundant food source.*

7

THE EFFICIENT FEEDER

THE CHOCOLATE-COLORED BEAR EMERGED FROM A *thicket of alders and shuffled onto a low grassy hill at the edge of a salt marsh. A backdrop of snowcapped peaks and icy glaciers rimmed the north side of the flats while gentle ocean waves lapped at the sand beaches to the south. Acres and acres of meadows intersected by numerous tidal guts stretched in front of the bear.*

Grazing brown bears dotted the green fields like cows in a pasture. Sows with cubs, large old boars, and small single bears, twenty-two in all, were methodically nibbling mouthfuls of short sedge. Occasionally they lifted their heads to chew, scanning the immediate surroundings before moving forward to continue grazing. Several bears with their bellies full of the rich green fiber slept peacefully. A large boar and a sow stood firmly coupled at the edge of the flats, for it was late spring and the breeding season was in full swing.

The chocolate male left the knoll and moved out to join the others. Ample room and food gave the contented bears little reason for confrontation.

As the morning progressed, a few bears returned to the alder thickets to rest while newcomers arrived. The chocolate bear fed for over an hour before he and two others quit grazing and moved toward the ocean beach. The morning tide had ebbed, exposing enormous sandbars that contained an abundance of razor clams. The majority of the bears left the meadows and scattered across the sandbars.

The chocolate male waded through a shallow lagoon left by the retreating tide and strode across the mud and sand flats, leaving a trail of footprints. He sniffed the ground, then stopped and began to dig with his forepaw. A mound of sand grew under his belly before he raked out a six-inch razor clam. With delicate and precise movements, he pried it open with two claws and licked out the contents. He moved a few feet, then repeated the action, this time crushing the clam with his teeth to gain access to the tasty morsel.

In time, thirty to forty holes littered with shell remains revealed his efficiency in digging. As the water receded, more bears arrived for breakfast. Gulls discovered the digging bears and swooped in to grab any uneaten tidbits.

The bears and gulls continued to feed for several hours until the incoming tide forced them back to higher ground. They followed a routine established eons ago, long before humans copied their behavior with their trusty clam shovels.

———————————

Bears are omnivorous and opportunistic feeders: their diet varies greatly from one small geographic area to another. They will consume grasses, sedges, roots, berries, fish, rodents, insects, large mammals, carrion, and garbage—whatever is available. Brown bears are usually portrayed as fish eaters in films and popular literature; they spend far more time, however, grazing on berries and green plants. They like a diverse diet and may abandon a plentiful food supply to find less abundant delicacies simply for a change of menu.

In general, the coastal brown bears' food habits are seasonal. During hibernation the stomachs of bears contract to a very small size, and when they first leave their winter dens, they have rather picky eating habits. Brownies often wander to lower elevations and beaches to search for new green shoots and carrion. They also dig for roots and will take the sand fleas that are abundant in kelp piles. As their appetites gradually return, the bears consume larger quantities of food.

In the spring they seek out grassy meadows and often congregate in large numbers. Brown bears graze much like cattle, grabbing mouthfuls of grass as they slowly move along to feed, stopping periodically to chew and swallow. Quite often they lie on their stomachs and graze lazily, sliding forward on their bellies to take more mouthfuls. Along parts of the Alaska Peninsula, sedge meadows are particularly prevalent, and if enough bears are present, they may keep the sedges cropped short by constant feeding, preferring the short, succulent vegetation over mature stands.

On portions of Kodiak Island, bears come together on high alpine slopes to feed on a different plant, the Alaska long-awned sedge (*Carex macrochaeta*). They may remain on these alpine areas through much of June and July, eating the new shoots that emerge as the snows recede. John Schoen reported that in Southeast Alaska some bears, especially females, may remain on alpine and steep avalanche slopes all summer and never descend to the lower elevations to feed on salmon. Bears eat many other new green plants such as horsetail, cow parsnip, nettle, beach rye grass, seaside angelica (*Angelica lucida*, also called seacoast celery), and, in Southeast Alaska, skunk cabbage. They consume an enormous quantity of vegetative material when it is available, and the meadows where they assemble to graze are strewn with piles of dung that resemble horse manure in a farm pasture.

Salmon become available in June in some coastal regions, but not until August in other areas. Fish is a favorite food item of bears, who prefer it to green vegetation when it is obtainable. Bears seem to have an uncanny ability to sense the arrival of salmon and often gather on the streams within a few days after the fish appear. Where salmon are evenly distributed, bears space themselves apart, and few confrontations take place. In places where rock falls, logjams, and other impediments exist, however, bears concentrate to fish. This crowding can result in disputes and, at times, even serious fights.

Brown bears have a difficult time capturing salmon in deep water. For this reason, voluminous rivers that contain millions of migrating salmon may receive very little bear activity. Bears are capable of successfully catching salmon only when fish

FIGURE 29   *Brown bears are omnivorous and feed on vegetation much of the year. This bear feeds on greens at Swikshak River marsh area in Katmai National Park.*

reach the shallow headwaters or tributaries of these large rivers.

Brownies seem to enjoy fishing, and their success usually increases with experience. Though methods may vary, they generally pounce on a fish with their forepaws, seize it with their teeth, and then move to a gravel bar or riverbank to consume their catch. Watching them fish is a popular sport for nature lovers; it can be humorous as well as exciting. Young bears often gallop up and down streams in vain, scattering salmon helter-skelter. Older, more experienced bears wade into shallow waters, stand and wait, and then make their catch by pouncing when a fish swims near.

FIGURE 30   *In some regions brown bears become proficient at digging clams. A red fox enjoys morsels left by this bear digging razor clams at Hallo Bay, Katmai National Park.*

Brown bears may use different techniques to fish around natural barriers where fish congregate in huge pools before continuing up the river. Some bears sit on rocks, snatching fish in midair as they attempt to leap the falls. Others sit in the water at the bottom of the falls, making a swift grab when they feel a salmon swim into them. Old bears are very patient: I have seen them sit for an hour at Brooks River Falls waiting for a fish to come close enough to make a catch. Some bears develop unusual fishing techniques. Once I watched a mature male sit at the edge of a stream that flowed into a small lake. Red salmon congregated in a deep pool below him. He watched and waited until a large school of fish filled the pool, then pounced like a cat, diving into the pool to make a catch. When he was not successful, he climbed back on his perch and waited for another school to congregate before taking another plunge.

Young, inexperienced bears may spend thirty minutes or more trying to make a catch. When successful, they literally strut from the stream with the salmon held high, as if to say, "Hey, look at the fish I caught." In this respect they are not much different from a young boy who has just caught his first fish on a rod.

Berries ripen in late summer, and some bears will leave the salmon streams to feed on blueberries, crowberries, salmonberries, high-bush cranberries, and a few other varieties. On Kodiak Island in late August they especially seek out the plentiful elderberries. For the next month, most bears feed in the berry thickets even though plenty of salmon remain in the streams. Along the Katmai Coast, however, few elderberries grow and thus are not as important for nourishment.

Bears eat berries by stripping them from bushes with their lips and mouths. They often bring their forepaws into play by bending taller bushes toward them while sitting on their haunches. Many of the berries pass through the bears' digestive systems whole, and their scats may be quite colorful. A friend of mine once found nice red piles of high-bush cranberries lying on a beach on Kodiak Island. She thought someone had been picking berries and had dumped them out; she couldn't understand why anyone would have done that. I asked her if she had gathered them, but she replied that she had not because her husband was hunting deer and they had enough food in camp. Suppressing a smile, I told her how the berries got on the beach. Her face twisted into a sick look; I am sure they were glad that they had not been in need of food.

Bears also dig and consume several species of mollusk, including cockles, blue mussels, and others. They particularly relish the shellfish in spring and early summer before salmon become available. Along the Alaska Peninsula and especially the Katmai Coast, extensive beds of razor clams thrive in the soft sandy tide flats. During the low tides of May, June, and July, large numbers of bears are often seen far offshore, feasting on razors. I have spent many hours watching bears locate and dig the shellfish. They walk slowly across the flats with their noses close to the surface. When a bear catches the scent or spots a dimple, it stops and digs very rapidly with its claws, excavating a small round hole. It may rake out the bivalve with its claws, or dig down a foot or two, then thrust its head into the hole and extract the clam by gripping it between its teeth. The bear may crush the shell with its teeth and lick out the meat. Sometimes it uses two or three claws to delicately pull the shell apart, exposing the contents. Occasionally a bear lays the clam down on the beach and crushes the shell by stomping on it.

Some bears become very efficient diggers, whereas the efforts of others are futile. Comical to watch, they often lean on a front elbow while digging deep holes with the other paw. Some are exclusively right-handed diggers, while others are left-handed. At times they thrust their heads into the holes; when they resurface, their faces are masks of mud. They can get annoyed, chasing gulls or red foxes that are waiting nearby to sneak their catch. A successful bear may dig fifty to one hundred razors in one low-tide period.

Bears also rake out and eat sand lance. These small fish, three to six inches in length, burrow under the surface of the sand when the tide is out. Though small, they provide a juicy tidbit.

Bears learn about food sources from their mothers or other bears, but they may also accidentally come across something new. Once they discover when and where a supply of food occurs, they never forget. Each spring along the coast of Katmai, bears swim out to certain islands that are inhabited by nesting gulls, apparently remembering which islands are occupied by gulls and when the egg-laying season occurs. I have found bears on islands that are a mile or more offshore. They remain for several days to a week gorging on omelets. They also feed on the young chicks.

When available, herring eggs, ants, and a variety of insects are other edibles. Herring deposit their eggs on kelp leaves near shore; when the tide is out, bears search the beaches and readily eat the egg-laden kelp leaves. They will also overturn rocks looking for copepods.

Brown bears also walk beaches looking for live or dead marine mammals. In the summer of 1978 I found a dead gray whale washed up on the beach in Hallo Bay on the Alaska Peninsula. Eighteen bears were in the vicinity when I first sighted it, and twelve were feeding on the carcass at any one time. I landed my floatplane and watched them for more than an hour. All the bears were singles except one sow with two cubs. The single bears spaced themselves evenly around the carcass, but every so often small squabbles erupted, forcing a few bears to leave. In time, they or others took up the vacated positions. The sow with the cubs never did feed when I was present; apparently she did not want to endanger her cubs with all those hungry single bears. I checked the carcass several times during the course of a week and approximately the same number of bears was always present. A high tide finally carried the dead whale out to sea and ended the feast.

Unfenced garbage dumps can also become favorite feeding areas for bears. Such trash sites are common around some Alaska communities and can be a major problem because they attract bears to people. Bear scats around such facilities attest to the bears' assorted diets. They contain almost every human food item available, plus plastic sacks, cloth, and various scraps of junk.

In some areas, newborn caribou, sheep, moose, and other ungulates become an important food source for a few weeks each spring (see chapter 10). Bears occasionally take adult animals as well, usually the sick or injured; healthy animals have a better chance of escaping. When bears cannot eat their kill in one day they bury the remains. They may drag the carcass to a secluded spot and cover it with grass, brush, moss, or whatever vegetative material is available, forming a huge mound. With their front claws they scrape the material onto the carcass much as a domestic cat covers its waste. Bears may bed down directly on top of the carcass or hide nearby to guard the food cache. When hunger strikes, they uncover all or part of the meat in order to feed, and then again bury the kill. This routine of eating and recovering continues until all that remains is the skeleton and hide.

CHAPTER SEVEN

FIGURE 31   *A young bear feeds on barnacles in Kukak Bay, Katmai National Park.*

Berries and fish are the main staple in the late fall and early winter just before bears hibernate. Many of the salmon taken late in the season are spawned-out, dead fish that are partially decomposed. Bears prefer the least-decayed fish and will search selectively for them if they have a choice. I have watched bears feeding at Brooks River late in October when few fresh fish were available. They frequently picked up and examined three or four badly decomposed salmon before choosing the one least deteriorated.

Late fall food sources are extremely important to bears because they need to gain ample fat reserves in order to survive the long hibernation period. In regions where late salmon runs are available, bears tend to hibernate later than in areas where salmon disappear earlier. These late salmon runs are thus critical for the well-being of bear populations.

Most people think salmon are bears' primary source of food. Yet while fish are certainly important in the brown bear diet, they are available only seasonally. In fact, bears require a great variety of entrees on their omnivorous menu, as well as a vast area containing different ecological zones to supply these foods. Like any hunter-gatherer, human or animal, bears must travel far and wide to collect their meals. When we understand the complexity of brown bear diet and travel, we see the critical importance of protecting the habitat that supplies all these resources.

FIGURE 32   *Bears often den on high mountain slopes that remain covered all winter, such as near the Kaguyak Crater area in Katmai National Park.*

8

THE LONG SLEEP

THE YOUNG SOW WADDLED AS SHE AMBLED ALONG *the shores of Brooks Lake, for she was extremely fat. Late October had arrived and since July she had been gorging herself on the abundant supply of red salmon. She would be six years old in February and was now a full-grown adult weighing nearly six hundred pounds.*

The brownie did not know why she had decided to leave Brooks River that morning and head toward Dumpling Mountain where she had spent the previous three winters. Perhaps it was the cold weather that had crept over her domain the past week, or the light snow that had fallen the previous day, or the disappearance of the salmon from the river. She had found a few spawned-out carcasses of red salmon in recent weeks, but these were decomposed and had little food value.

She followed an old bear trail through the forest, stopping occasionally to graze on some ripe highbush cranberries under the tall cottonwood trees. When the young sow reached the base of the mountain, she lay down in a patch of grass and slept until early afternoon. As she continued her slow, deliberate shuffle up the mountain, she passed through groves of spruce, cottonwood, birch, and alder.

Just before dark the sow found a slight depression on a small knoll and bedded down for the night. The young female was content to rest at an elevation of 1,700 feet where she had a sweeping view of the rivers, lakes, and meadows below. She had roamed the area during the past few months, mostly alone but occasionally in contact with other bears. She had expended considerable effort trying to avoid the humans that seemed to be everywhere along the Brooks River.

The next morning she got up, stretched, and watched several bald eagles circling near her bed. She nibbled on some crowberries before continuing up the steep slope for another hundred feet to the base of a large alder bush. The bear sniffed the ground for a few minutes, and then with her powerful claws began to rip up grass roots and small bushes. Large chunks of dirt and rocks went rolling down the hill. She clawed and ripped a hole about three feet into the mountain, creating a small mound below her. When her claws scraped across a boulder, she tried to remove it by digging on each side of the huge rock, but the powerful bear was unable to budge it. This made her angry, and for a few minutes she dug with a vengeance on the far left side of the boulder. Making little progress, she slapped at it in disgust and emitted a gruff grunt. She backed out of the shallow hole and stood looking downhill.

The bear scraped a level spot on the mound of dirt for a day bed and lay down to contemplate the wasted effort. After a few restless minutes, she skirted the mountain for a hundred yards to the base of another alder bush.

The brownie began to dig again with her powerful paws, slowly then rapidly, sending rocks and dirt flying down the forty-degree incline. By dark she had excavated a hole deep into the hillside about three feet in diameter, large enough so that she could easily crawl inside. She retreated to the day bed at her first excavation and scraped in some grass and moss before lying down for the night.

The bear slept little, restlessly turning over many times. Before dawn she returned and resumed her digging, enlarging the den. She alternately dug and rested as the hole and the mound of dirt grew. By evening the den was complete. She was tired; she lay down and fell asleep. The chamber measured approximately seven feet long, five feet wide, and three feet high.

During the next few days the brownie slept, chewed off alder twigs, and scraped up grass and moss to line her den. Sometimes she visited the mound next to the first den site to sleep and rest, but then she returned to her newly dug den, disappearing inside for a few hours. Each day her movements *became slower and she spent more time resting. On the fifth day the sow disappeared into her den for the last time and fell asleep. Her heart rate and breathing slowed markedly. Her body temperature also dropped, but the small chamber remained at a comfortable temperature.*

She now lay in a sleeping stupor and would remain so for the next six months. She would live off her large reserves of stored fat, without eating, drinking, urinating, or defecating. The young sow was in a state of hibernation and would remain oblivious to the stormy winds and snow that swirled outside her den during the cold winter months.

———————

Animal hibernation has always been a fascinating and mysterious phenomenon surrounded by many misconceptions. Perhaps people have envied an animal's ability to spend the cold, harsh winter months peacefully slumbering away, while humans are forced to fight the elements. Since little factual information on hibernation has been available, the myths grew. With modern technology, however, scientists have recently been able to follow hibernators to their dens and unravel many of the secrets of this unique behavior.

Many biologists believe brown bears are not true hibernators during the denning period, but instead enter a state of deep dormancy. Their heart and respiration rates are greatly reduced, much like those of the small mammal hibernators, such as ground squirrels and marmots. The true hibernator's body temperature is reduced until it approaches the temperature of its surroundings; the body temperature of bears, however, is lowered by only a few degrees inside their winter dens. This adaptation often permits bears to become quickly aroused if disturbed.

Some people have found this out too late, to their misfortune. One spring several years ago an Anchorage newspaper reported that two hunters had tried to prod a bear from its den with long sticks. The bear came out, to be sure, but in a mad rush, killing both hunters before they could defend themselves with rifles.

During the winter dormant period, bears live on the fat reserves accumulated each fall prior to entering the den, and thus lose a substantial amount of weight. They maintain bone growth, and females with newborn cubs produce rich milk that feeds their young for several months in the den. Brown bears typically den on high mountain slopes that are well drained and snow covered during most of the winter. The elevation of the den site, the steepness of the slope, and the orientation of the dens vary considerably from one geographic region to another.

Biologists have studied denning habits in depth, and they vary in different areas. Jim Faro and I conducted an aerial denning survey in the Katmai region in May 1974. The bears had already emerged from their dens or were still around the entrance during this period. We found 232 dens; 70 percent were between 900 and 1,500 feet in elevation, and the highest was 2,800 feet above sea level. Fifty-two percent of these faced south; the remainder faced north, east, and west in approximately equal numbers. We also found that most of the dens were dug into well-drained slopes of twenty to thirty-five degrees.

FIGURES 33–34   *Dick Hensel examining vacated bear dens in the Kodiak National Wildlife Refuge.*

FIGURE 35   *Bears usually den on well-drained mountain slopes, such as this one in Becharof National Wildlife Refuge.*

Vic Barnes, Roger Smith, and Lawrence Van Daele conducted extensive studies on the denning habits of radio-collared bears in two different areas on Kodiak Island. They reported that brownies denned at an average elevation of 2,180 feet above sea level in the northern study area, compared to 1,500 feet in the southwestern region. The highest recorded den site was at 3,900 feet. Slope orientation also varied in the two study areas. In other geographic regions of Alaska where mountains are higher, bears den at even greater elevations than those reported on Kodiak Island and the Alaska Peninsula.

Some bears also den at extremely low elevations. Jim Faro and I examined fourteen vacated dens on small, low islands in Becharof Lake, which is about fourteen feet above sea level. Many of these dens were just above the waterline of the lake. A large, late fall run of salmon spawn around the shores of these islands. Bear trails crisscross the islands, indicating that bears use them heavily during the late fall period. The bears seemed to be taking advantage of suitable den sites close to their late fall feeding ranges despite the fact that the dens were at a much lower elevation than they would normally use.

In popular literature, bears are always depicted as spending hibernation periods in natural rock caves. This is true in many regions such as Southeast Alaska where sites are available on steep, rocky slopes found on some high mountains. But natural rock caves are rare in many coastal areas of Alaska. Where caves are not available, bears dig dens into well-drained soils, usually at the base of an alder or willow bush so that the roots will help support the soils and keep the dens from collapsing. Most of the dens I have examined in the summer had already collapsed from melting snows and rains that eroded the soils.

Because of this erosion, bears are often forced to dig new dens each fall. Where rock dens are available or dens are dug in more stable soils, bears often use the same den year after year.

Some mountainsides seem to be teeming with bear dens, whereas others are nearly devoid of denning sites. Bears are opportunistic animals and will dig dens wherever the right conditions exist. I suspect that choosing and digging a den site is both an evolutionary instinct and a learned behavior. Cubs, while denning with their mother for one or two winters, may be taught suitable sites and types of habitat.

The period when bears enter dens in the fall also varies from region to region and by sex and age. Much depends on food availability in late fall, the length of seasons, outdoor temperatures, and perhaps snow depths. On Kodiak Island I always found that bears started disappearing rapidly after the first hard cold snap of November. Bears were abundant one week, then scarce the next. This change often coincided with the disappearance of the last salmon, but not always.

Most researchers agree that pregnant females are the first to enter dens in the fall, followed by lone females, and then females with young. Males, particularly the large old adults, are the last to hibernate. Biologists have reported that on the Alaska Peninsula pregnant females den around October 13, and males three days later; in Southeast Alaska the respective dates are October 22 and November 5. On Kodiak Island, researchers followed bears to their den sites with radios and monitored them for several years. They found that dates of entrance and emergence varied from year to year and from one geographical portion of the island to another, depending on temperatures, food supplies, and other factors. In northern Kodiak most pregnant females entered dens around November 5, but not until November 19 in southwestern Kodiak. Males were the last to enter dens; on average they entered on November 16 in the north and December 12 in the southwest. A few bears never den during mild winters along the maritime coast of Alaska. Those that I have seen out late in the season always appeared lean and emaciated. Clearly, they were having a difficult time finding enough food to sustain themselves.

In southwestern Alaska dens usually consist of an entrance tunnel and a chamber in which one or more bears spend the winter. Tunnels are typically oval or arch-shaped and around three feet in diameter. They are normally several feet in length and lead directly into the chamber, the floor of which is usually lower than the tunnel. The size of the chamber varies, depending upon the size and number of bears involved, but averages around seven feet long, four to six feet wide, and three to four feet high. In other words, the entrance tunnel and chamber are easily large enough for a human to climb into. I have done this a number of times—in the summer after the den was vacated, of course!

Bears often use alder branches, grass, and moss as bedding material. I first became aware of this when I read through some unpublished field notes taken by my colleague Earl Fleming. He reported the following sequence of events gleaned from watching a bear prepare for hibernation:

> *November 8, 1962.* Located a bear sitting near mouth of a large hole. Bear sat for an hour, then moved 40 feet and appeared to dig for mice; entered den and remained for 30 minutes. Last seen at dark lying in snow at entrance.

> *November 9.* Bear lay prostrate at den entrance most of day.

> *November 10.* Bear sits or lies at mouth of den entrance; occasionally picks up snow and grass and slowly chews contents like cow chewing cud. In afternoon moves approximately 50 feet to alder growths and while sitting on hind legs begins taking alder branches in paws and chews off small twigs.

> *November 11.* Bear stands at entrance upon huge mound of dirt piled in front of entrance. Stands with head hanging down or gazes into space for long periods. Bear enters den and resumes excavating as stones and dirt are thrown from den.

> *November 13.* Bear consumes a considerable amount of snow, then enters den; observation terminated.

Later, after I had crawled into several dens and found them lined with alder branches and grass, I concluded that the bear Earl watched was gathering vegetative materials for its bed, even though Earl had never seen it carrying them in.

The time of den emergence in the spring also varies by sex and age. Nearly all researchers agree that males are the first to leave their dens, followed by single females, and then females with young. The last to leave are sows with the newborn cubs, who typically come out during the last two weeks in May, but often not until June. In areas where pregnant females enter dens early, they also leave at a slightly earlier date. Average den emergence for males is around March 8 in southwestern Kodiak Island and April 22 in northern Kodiak and the Alaska Peninsula. The males appear to spend from three to five months in their dens, whereas pregnant females may spend up to seven months in hibernation.

When bears awake from their long winter sleep they tend to be sluggish and their bodily functions take time to return to normal. Quite soon after emerging, they pass a fecal plug, possibly one or two feet in length. It consists of food material that has accumulated in the lower part of the intestine, the result of not eating or defecating all winter. Several days may pass before the newly awakened bears wander to lower elevations and gradually begin to feed on new plant shoots or whatever else is available. Sows with newborn cubs usually remain at the denning site for a week or two, continuing to use the inside of the den for rest and sleep. This permits the cubs to adapt gradually to the outside world.

Without a period of hibernation, bears would be forced to compete for the limited amount of food that would be available during the long winter months, the result of which would be an increase in conflict, a decrease in bear survival, and a decrease in the size of bear populations. Thus bears' ability to hibernate or enter a period of dormancy is a strategy of adaptation that serves them well.

FIGURE 36   *Mothers of single cubs may spend hours playing with their offspring.*

PLAY AND PERCEPTION

TWO YOUNG SIBLINGS WERE FISHING THE BROOKS *River early one morning. Fishing was effortless in late September because the river was still full of red salmon. Many were spawned out, lethargic, and easy to catch.*

The bears had entered the river above Brooks Falls and gradually worked their way downstream. Sometimes they fed side by side; at other times they briefly separated as they worked the middle of the river or walked the banks. Occasionally they detoured around the larger bears they feared.

By six o'clock they were on the lower river and full of fish. Junior, the young male, left the river, followed by his older sister. They walked across a small meadow, climbed onto a knoll, and lay down to rest, contented.

Before long, Sister walked over to Junior. She began to mouth his ears and gently cuff his head, eager to play. Roused by her efforts, Junior jumped up and threw a leg over her shoulder. In a moment they were both on their hind legs, locked in a bear hug and shoving each other back and forth, growling and biting. At times they may have appeared to be fighting, but the thick fur and hide prevented injury.

The wrestling continued for fifteen minutes, and then abruptly Junior broke it off and started to wander along the riverbank. Sister galloped after him. They frolicked and ran through the spruce trees, following a trail to a gravel road.

As they approached the edge of the road, Sister spotted a brown post. It had been placed there by the park rangers to mark a foot trail for tourists. She reared up and grabbed the post with her paws, attempting to shake it without success. Sister then reached up and tore out a big chunk of wood with her teeth. Not to be outdone, Junior stood on his hind legs and grabbed the sign that said TRAIL; with a twisting yank, he ripped it down. He ran down the road with the sign in his mouth and quickly destroyed it.

The two continued romping toward Naknek Lake. They were feeling frisky and looking for more entertainment. As they approached Brooks Camp, they saw a rubber raft on the beach. The siblings walked around it, sniffing the contents. Sister grabbed a rope in her teeth and tugged and jerked on it before placing her paws on top of the boat and leaping inside. The two bears began pulling and chewing on anything they could find. Junior sank his teeth into a plastic bucket, which flipped over his head. Alarmed, he shook his head, flinging the bucket aside. Sister bit into the side of the raft, puncturing the rubber tube. The loud whooshing sound of escaping air sent the pair running for the shore of the lake.

They came to the Brooks Lake campground, filled with campers. Tents were scattered about under the cottonwood and spruce trees. As they approached the first one, Sister grabbed a tent rope. She jerked and yanked until the tent was flapping in every direction. This was her undoing, because the camper inside awoke and let out a bloodcurdling scream. The sudden noise startled the mischievous bears. Snorting and huffing, they galloped through the campground, stumbling over several tent ropes. Sleepy campers awoke and rushed from their tents, screaming and yelling "Bears! Bears!" and "Get out of here!"

A few campers began to beat pots and pans just as the rangers had told them to do. The sudden loud racket and the people running hither and yon frightened the young bears as they ran for their lives. They did not stop running until they reached a thick patch of brush where they could hide. The siblings did not realize they had given the campers an exciting experience to talk about for days to come.

lay is an important part of a young brown bear's life just as it is with many other mammal species, including humans. Young cubs spend a lot of time playing with each other. Watching a litter of two or three cubs is a peaceful, wild, entertaining experience as they roughhouse, box, bite, and rear up on hind legs, batting and flailing at one another with their small paws.

The mother often watches the cubs calmly, but occasionally she too is brought into the games if she is lying down and they start romping on her back or stomach. She may push them around with her paws as they tussle and run over her, playing hide and seek, or "Let's bite Momma's ear."

Young cubs sometimes use objects to entertain themselves. On many occasions I have seen cubs play with sticks, rocks, or other materials. If the stick is large, they may try to stand it on end, then rear up on hind legs to grab the top or perform some other contortion, which often results in falling over backward. They love to climb on logs, walk out on an extended limb until they tumble to the ground, and then repeat the performance.

As the cubs grow, play becomes rougher. Siblings that have been weaned and other juvenile bears will meet and often wrestle. Bears cautiously approach one another, nose to nose, then begin mouthing and chewing on each other's ears, head, and neck. After a few minutes, the action escalates. Typically one bear will throw a foreleg over the other's shoulder until they are both on their hind legs, locked in an embrace and shoving, growling, and biting. What an experience it is to watch two fairly large brown bears tussling in simulated fighting. One often gets knocked to the ground, kicking and biting, but soon both are up again, rising on their hind legs to lock together like two struggling wrestlers. Such roughhousing may last for thirty minutes or

more before one bear gets tired, breaks off the play, and then turns and runs away.

Bears find various other opportunities to entertain themselves. They are noted for their love of playing with man-made equipment and consequently can become real pests when they come in contact with the human environment. In a few minutes they may tear down signs or rip up boats and tents, just for fun. They can quickly demolish the inside of a cabin, as many people who live in bear country have learned. Sometimes they do it in search of food, but often meddling bears are just enjoying themselves.

Early one morning I watched a young male sauntering along a stream filled with splashing salmon. His belly filled with fish, he appeared to be bored and looking for amusement. He came to a red salmon lying dead on a gravel bar and grabbed the fish by the tail with his teeth. He carried it for a few yards, then snapped his head and gave it a mighty fling across the gravel bar. He ran to where the fish landed, again grabbed the tail and gave it another heave. It sailed through the air and landed in some tall grass. Finding the salmon, he walked out to the gravel bar and repeated the performance. After six or seven rounds, he finally tired of the game.

Bears like to rest on snow patches to keep cool during hot summer days. If the snow is on a steep slope, they often roll and slide down the slippery surface, bodysurfing with gusto. I have often seen them skidding on their backs, then turning over, rolling and tumbling as they slip down the mountain. When they reach the bottom of the snow slide, the entertainment usually ends, though I have seen bears climb back up to the top of the snow patch to repeat the sliding game.

The guide Morris Talifson told me that he once watched a sow with a yearling cub descend a

FIGURE 37   *Yearling cubs spend many hours playing and wrestling.*

mountain on Kodiak Island in late May. Fresh snow had fallen and the temperature was fairly mild. Apparently moisture conditions were ideal for forming snowballs. As the sow shuffled along the mountainside, several clumps of snow broke loose and enlarged as they rolled down the slope. After they came to rest, the bear was attracted to the largest snowball. Placing her paws on the ball, she rolled it a short distance. This continued until the ball became sizable and dropped into a small ravine. When she could not budge it by her usual methods, the sow lay down, placed her hind feet against it, and pushed, to no avail. This seemed to arouse her anger, for she jumped up and began swatting the snowball with her front paws until it was completely shattered.

Dick Hensel entertained me with his observation of a young brownie wading down a stream until it came to a fallen cottonwood tree blocking the stream. Five magpies were perched on a limb that protruded about ten feet above the top of the downed trunk. The birds made a vocal issue of the bear's presence, and it became annoyed at their noisy clamor. The young bear stepped onto the fallen tree and walked to the limb supporting the obnoxious five. It shook the branch until four of the birds took flight; the noise of the remaining magpie increased loudly. The young bruin, without a change in stance, ceased shaking the limb and stared persistently at the agitator. After a pause, the animal resumed shaking the limb with increasing tempo until finally the magpie could not hang onto its perch any longer. This restored silence to the calm day, and the contented bear continued its travels downstream, perhaps thinking, "Well, I sure fixed those noisy rascals!"

Even though play diminishes with age, sows that have single cubs play for long periods with their offspring. A mother will use her huge paws to push the cub or gently mouth the youngster. Lying on her back, she lets the cub romp over her while she pushes it around. Bear mothers seem to realize that they have to entertain their young when no littermates exist. In Hallo Bay two sows with single cubs seemed to solve this problem by letting their cubs play together while they fed nearby on sedges or salmon. Apparently they trusted each other.

Young cubs and yearlings climb trees quite readily and can shinny up to considerable heights while playing or trying to escape danger. Adult bears usually do not climb trees, but will occasionally go up into the lower part of a large leaning tree. Early one morning on Kodiak Island, I was sitting on a high ridge overlooking O'Malley River when I spotted a young bear of 350 pounds or so walking along the riverbank. It had completed its fishing for the morning and appeared to be bored and looking for something to do. As the animal walked along, it occasionally bit off a willow limb, and then dropped it, apparently for amusement. It approached a young cottonwood tree about twelve inches in diameter and thirty feet in height. The branches were evenly spread at two- or three-foot intervals. As the bear came to the tree, it stood erect, placing its front feet on the lower branches. As I watched in amazement, it climbed from limb to limb as a man would ascend a ladder. At a height of about twenty feet, the brownie halted, bit off several branches an inch or two in diameter, looked around for a few minutes, and then backed down the tree. I could see no functional reason for the bear to climb; it simply was looking for entertainment or challenge: "I wonder if I can do it?"

Brown bears love to lie in streams to cool off in the summer. They are excellent swimmers and can easily cross lakes or bays that are a mile or more wide. They swim with their bodies low, head and nose only slightly above the waterline. Cubs learn early in life to swim and follow their mothers. Sometimes she leads them across dangerously swift rivers, though, and the young cubs are not always adept in dealing with the currents. Occasionally they are swept downstream, becoming separated or even lost. Cubs often fear these crossings and bawl insistently, protesting to their mother that they do not wish to swim.

On several occasions I have watched cubs follow the sow closely while swimming. When the opportunity arises, they manage to climb up on their mother and ride piggyback. Usually they slide down when she reaches land, but sometimes they continue to ride for a while as she grazes. The cubs may also crawl on their mother's back while she is resting or sleeping, remaining there when she gets up and walks away. Like human kids, they apparently enjoy the ride.

Bears are not only capable of swimming, but some have learned to dive underwater to feed on salmon. Others are good snorkelers as they wade in rivers or lakes with their heads and eyes below the surface in search of fish.

At Brooks River, a large male was named Diver by the rangers and biologists because he was adept at diving for salmon. Diver was a mature boar and already had this habit and reputation when I began doing research at Brooks in the mid-1970s. During a subsequent visit in 1989 I saw him again. He was very large, quite old, and his body was covered with battle scars, but he was still performing his diving act. He dove underwater headfirst, then his rear end rose high before it, too, disappeared porpoise-style.

When bears are not playing or feeding, they spend a lot of time resting and sleeping. They often lie out on an open knoll, snoozing for several hours before getting up and wandering out to feed again. They prefer resting on elevated spots where they can watch the surroundings. Much of their inactive period, however, is spent in well-hidden alder patches, lying in day beds. Bears often scoop out these shallow depressions with their front paws. They may curl up inside the beds or lie with paws and head extended over the edge. They often pose in comical positions, such as lying on their backs with all four feet in the air. Well-used day beds are abundant in areas of dense bear concentrations.

While the antics of bears are fun to watch, bears are often difficult to approach because of their keen senses. Popular belief has it that brown bears have poor eyesight, but I disagree. I think people tend to measure their own sensory perception skills against those of all other creatures. Since we depend primarily on eyesight to distinguish distant objects, we measure an animal's vision against our own. If their sighting capability is less than ours, we rate it as poor. On the other hand, we are astounded at many animals' ability to locate things by smell, because our sense of smell is relatively limited. I have often tried to approach a bear upwind through an open meadow, only to have it run from me when I was still several hundred yards away. I was sure it could not detect me by smell. Bears quickly become aware of moving objects at a great distance. Just try to approach a bear by boat along a lakeshore. One soon finds that the animal can spot the moving boat on the water at extreme distances, running away if it is not used to seeing boats.

The bear's sense of smell is unusually keen; it often relies on scent to verify what it thinks it sees. Thus a bear, upon sighting a person, may look intently for a few minutes, then circle downwind to verify with its nose what it saw with its eyes. It sniffs the air with its supersensitive nose. Brown bears frequently stand on their hind legs to get a better view of something they have detected. The extra height

FIGURE 38   *This bear rests in a pool of water to keep cool.*

FIGURE 39   *Bears stand on their hind legs to see better.*

gives them an advantage to use their senses. When it detects the dreaded scent, the bear reacts, seeming to say, "Yep, it's a person. I'd better run!"

Bears depend also upon their noses to locate most of their food. They can detect odors such as a dead animal for a distance of a mile or more if the wind is blowing in the right direction. They can also scent a trail of an animal, a human, or another bear that may be several hours old and easily follow it. During the breeding season, males seem to distinguish between the scent trail of a female and that of a male—they will not waste their time following a male's trail when they are looking for a mate. Their sense of smell is approximately equal to, or better than, that of a good bird dog.

Hearing is also acute and bears are able to detect noises at extreme distances. While conducting aerial bear surveys I often saw them react to and run from my noisy airplane when I was still a mile away. If you are trying to sneak up on bears, for example to take photographs, even the slightest crack of a twig brings them to an alert stance. They may spook from a noise without verifying the sound with their other senses.

Sensory perceptions of bears often decrease with age just as they do in humans. Finding really old bears that can barely see or hear is not unusual, but their sense of smell does not seem to diminish.

Playing, wrestling, and other antics performed by young bears are very entertaining to watch, to be sure. And these interactions are no doubt fun for the juveniles as well—but they are also learning how to defend themselves and to find their places in the complex society of bears.

FIGURE 40   *Salmon are an important food source for most coastal brown bears. This bear is catching fish in Brooks Falls at Naknek Lake, Katmai National Park.*

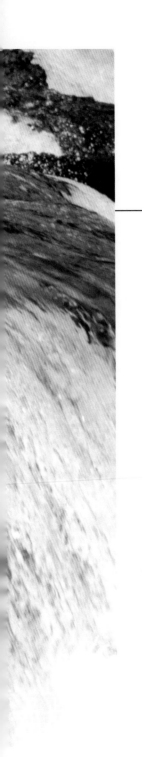

10

THE BEAR AS PREDATOR

THE BLOND SOW AND HER TWO YEARLING CUBS FED *all morning on the new green plants that grew profusely along the shores of Naknek Lake. For the past three weeks the family had remained in a two-square-mile area, sometimes grazing on the edge of the lake and at other times wandering a mile inland onto the lower slopes of a mountainside where an abundance of fresh vegetation grew. The core of the family's feeding area was a one-half-mile strip of grassy meadow that lay a hundred yards inland from the lake. Dense stands of alder and willow thickets and an occasional birch tree surrounded it.*

Their daily pattern was to feed in the early morning, and then at about ten o'clock drift into the alders to rest for several hours before continuing to graze. An ample supply of herbage filled their bellies, but the blond sow longed for some meat to supplement their diet. The family's only meat since leaving the den had been the partial remains of a moose that had starved in late winter. Fox, magpies, and ravens had got to it first and only scraps remained for the bears. Blondie saw several moose and gave chase, but her efforts were futile.

One spring morning in June, a cow moose with week-old twin calves swam ashore from a small island in the lake. They fed on some new willow tips and horsetail on the northeast side of the meadow, but never strayed far from the alders.

While Blondie and her two cubs were munching greens two days later, a light northeast breeze blew directly toward the bears. The sow stopped grazing; her sensitive nose had caught the scent of moose. She stood alert for a long time sucking air through her nostrils. The yearlings also sensed something unusual and moved to her side. All three rose to their hind legs, sniffing the air for a few minutes. Blondie gave a short grunt and began to move along the edge of the alders with her cubs at heel. Every hundred yards or so she stopped to sniff the air, and then cautiously advanced. She stopped toward the end of the meadow, stood up, and saw the cow moose step in front of an alder bush to feed. The calves emerged from the brush to stand close by.

With a grunt signal, Blondie directed her cubs to wait, and then began a stealthy stalk. The moose continued to eat, unaware that potential disaster was approaching. Blondie crept forward fifty yards, then waited behind a dense shrub. The cow moose and her calves slowly fed toward the sow in the meadow. A step or two at a time, they closed the gap. Blondie waited in anticipation, her muscles taut. When the moose got within forty yards, Blondie charged, hoping to cut off a calf. The cow was no coward and turned to face her potential killer; her ears lay back and the hair along her neck and shoulders stood erect. Blondie was unsure of herself and stopped to assess the situation. The cow stomped her feet and reared on her hind legs, threatening Blondie with her sharp hooves.

The sow now charged to the left, but the moose turned to face the challenge. Feinting one direction and then another, Blondie attempted to separate the twins from their mother, but the moose rushed between the bear and the calves each time. The sow kept up her consistent harassment until, for some unknown reason, the calves bolted, running in different directions. The cow placed herself in front of the nearest one. In a flash Blondie saw her opportunity, rushed past the cow, and in one quick swipe of her paws knocked the other calf off its feet, crushing its neck with her powerful jaws. The cow moose trotted away rapidly with her remaining offspring. Blondie uttered a few low woofs and the yearlings rushed to her side. The feast began.

rown bears in general are not highly successful in killing healthy adult moose, deer, and caribou; they are, however, very competent in taking young calves. According to some studies, they are responsible for killing up to half the moose calves born in certain areas. The situation depends upon the number of calves available and the number of bears present in a given range. Moose cows often defend their calves vigorously, but a bear can more easily separate twins and take at least one of them. Some bears become proficient at this skill. They learn to make quick feints and false charges at the moose until they divide the calves, and then the cow has to choose which of her offspring to protect as the bear easily kills the other. By the time calves are four weeks old, bears have a more difficult time.

Each year near my home on the Kenai Peninsula, several cow moose give birth. They seem aware that bears avoid the place. One evening in the spring of 1994, however, a wandering brownie arrived. A neighbor saw a bear chase a cow with twins into a forested ravine between our two homes. The next day we searched the draw and found the remains of the two-week-old calves. The bear had killed and eviscerated both, eating the insides and part of the front shoulders. Surprisingly, it had left both hindquarters intact.

Moose seem to have developed a protective behavior on the Kenai Peninsula. Cows often swim to the small islands in the numerous lakes to give birth. After the young are a few weeks old, the mother swims her offspring to the mainland. She thus avoids the bears when the calves are most vulnerable.

Bears also take a few young caribou and deer fawns. Generally, caribou calves gain the ability to run and keep up with the herd at a much earlier age than do moose and are therefore less vulnerable. Several years ago I saw a group of about fifty cow caribou feeding near a tundra pond on the Alaska Peninsula. While I watched, a brown bear walked out of some willows and caught the scent of the caribou. It started running toward the caribou, but they saw the bear and quickly outdistanced it. The brownie continued the pursuit, but each time it drew near, the caribou easily ran away from the bear. They seemed to be teasing it. After about thirty minutes, the brownie gave up and began to graze. The three-week-old calves kept up with the herd and were never threatened.

In early spring bears do occasionally take adult moose or caribou that are in poor physical condition, as well as during the fall rutting season when the bulls are fighting one another and are unwary. When a bear kills a large animal, it has enough food to last for some time.

In many coastal areas brown bears search the beaches for marine mammals. Most sea lions and walruses haul out on islands, but harbor seals often pull up on sandy beaches along the mainland. Bears can easily overtake these lumbering animals if they are far from saltwater.

FIGURE 41   *Harbor seals are easy prey for coastal brown bears.*

FIGURE 42   *Brown bears are capable of killing many mammals for food, from small mice to large moose. They are especially efficient at catching salmon, as demonstrated by this bear at Brooks River, Naknek Lake, Katmai National Park.*

Both brown bears and interior grizzlies prey on small mammals such as voles, ground squirrels, and marmots. I have watched them dig out huge boulders and mounds of dirt in pursuit of small mammals. Voles often elude bears after they have been evicted from their burrows, but make a tasty dessert when the bear gets lucky. I have never seen a brownie kill a porcupine, but I have seen bears with quills in their noses or mouths, indicating they must occasionally try.

On the Copper River Delta, brown bears are proficient at robbing goose nests and can have a serious impact on these birds. They do the same with nesting gulls. Sometimes adult gulls become victims when they get too close to a bear while trying to steal some of the bear's food. Brownies also relish the eggs and young of ground-nesting birds when the opportunity presents itself.

Only moderately successful in the taking of many species of birds and mammals, the brown bear is skilled and accomplished when it comes to preying on salmon. Its knowledge has been honed by centuries of experience, and its fishing methods passed down from generation to generation. Bear and salmon have coexisted along coastal Alaska since long before the arrival of modern humans.

Evidence of the successful relationship of the two species are the hordes of salmon that filled the rivers and streams in historical times.

Whenever humans, the most efficient predators of all, exploit a resource and drastically reduce its numbers, we have a habit of blaming the decline on competing predators. Dolly Varden trout are known to eat salmon eggs and young fry; bald eagles swoop down on streams and take salmon in plain sight for all to see. Seals are proficient killers of salmon and sometimes take them from fishing nets. So we tend to assume that some culprit other than ourselves must have caused the damage. In the western United States grizzlies and wolves were virtually eliminated because they competed with humans. Populations of coyotes, fox, eagles, and other predators were also dramatically reduced.

Likewise in Alaska, prior to statehood, the citizens of the territory blamed many predator species for reducing salmon population and the government placed bounties on them to reduce their numbers. Though bounties were never placed on bears in Alaska, the animals were blamed for the deterioration of salmon runs. Many fishermen who walked along Alaska's streams and saw the numerous, partly consumed carcasses strewn along the banks were convinced that bear predation must be a major factor in lower numbers of salmon. "Let's get rid of the bears" was the prevailing attitude. And fishermen shot them indiscriminately along the beaches.

Adding fuel to the fire was an article published in a prestigious journal in 1950 by Richard Schuman, a commercial fishery biologist, on the effect of bear predation on salmon. He reported that, at Karluk Lake on Kodiak Island during 1947, brown bears took a large number of red salmon, and concluded that immediate control of the bear population was urgently needed. Ironically, Karluk Lake was in the heart of the Kodiak National Wildlife Refuge, which had been established to protect bears.

Historically, Karluk Lake had contained the most productive red salmon waters on Kodiak Island. Commercial fishing began at the mouth of Karluk River in 1882, and for the next twenty-five years salmon were ruthlessly exploited. By 1889, the annual salmon harvest had increased to 3.4 million fish. Fishermen operated a fish trap at the mouth of Karluk River for many years and at times the river was completely blocked with nets. Commercial fishing took a high percentage of the run. As a result of overfishing, the red salmon population started a downward spiral. By the time Schuman conducted his studies in 1947, less than a million fish entered the river annually. (The fishery continued to decline further in succeeding years until the number entering Karluk Lake was below 200,000 salmon.)

Schuman conducted his study by placing a fish weir, a barrier that allows fish into the stream but not out, across the mouth of Moraine Creek. Each day he tallied the salmon as they passed up the stream to spawn. By classifying the fish carcasses that accumulated on the upstream side of the weir, he determined that, of the dead fish he examined, 31 percent were unspawned fish killed by bears. Applying these findings to the total population of red salmon in the Karluk Lake system, he concluded that bears had taken 94,119 unspawned red salmon.

Schuman's study contained many fallacies. For one, he studied only Moraine Creek, a small stream that flows into Karluk Lake. Eleven similar streams exist in the Karluk Lake system, but the majority of red salmon spawn in the two larger streams, Thumb and O'Malley, and along the lakeshores. Salmon are easy to catch in small, shallow lakeside streams, whereas bears are much less successful in deeper rivers and along lakeshores. Clearly, the stream he studied was not representative of salmon populations and bear predation in the area.

Schuman made another major error in designing his study. Salmon in small Karluk Lake streams have developed one very effective survival technique. When chased by bears, they rush downstream to escape into the deeper waters of Karluk Lake. Female salmon normally make several trips before completing their egg-laying. Schuman's weir blocked the salmon's escape route, thereby increasing the predation rate.

I have often watched bears fish in these shallow streams. As soon as a bear starts chasing salmon, the fish swim downstream en masse into the deeper lake. Sometimes a stream that has several hundred salmon becomes devoid of fish within a few minutes after bears appear. As a counter-strategy, bears may take advantage of a structure such as a weir by chasing the fish into the barrier where they are easily caught. In effect, Schuman's weir acted like a fence—funneling the fish, feeding the bears, and artificially inflating his results.

I know that Schuman believed in his studies and felt that reducing bear populations would help increase the waning numbers of salmon. In 1953 I heard him discuss in very intense and earnest language the merits of reducing bear populations. The language of his report also placed a tremendous amount of pressure on the Kodiak Refuge personnel and others who believed in the value and preservation of brown bears. To counter the bad publicity the bears got from Schuman's study and to check his questionable research, the refuge staff conducted additional, longer-term studies, one lasting

from 1950 through 1953 and a second from 1955 through 1956.

W. K. Clark and J. Lutz investigated predation on salmon in Karluk Lake and in other parts of Kodiak Island. Clark designed a weir that allowed red salmon to escape downstream and into a large holding pen in deeper waters. This simulated more natural conditions and avoided trapping the salmon in smaller streams as Schuman had done. Their findings indicated that unspawned salmon mortalities by bears were merely around one percent in most years.

Though such studies refuted much of what Schuman reported, the damage to bears had already been done. The first information to hit the news media, even if it is false and subsequently corrected, tends to make the most lasting impression on public consciousness. Many commercial cannery operators and fishermen who had been overexploiting the resources for decades heard what they wanted to hear: the bears were causing the decline of salmon in Alaska.

When I arrived at Kodiak as refuge manager in 1955 I redirected the research away from bear-salmon relationships and toward more positive studies of the life history and aesthetic values of the brown bear. Over the years we made considerable progress, and gradually the public image of brown bears began to change.

Fishery biologists continued to conduct bear-salmon studies during the 1960s that further disproved Schuman's conclusions. Ted Merrell, examining Brooks Lake, and W. R. Meehan, working in Southeast Alaska, both deduced that bears had little effect on salmon populations. Dick Gard evaluated bear predation in the Karluk Lake drainage that Schuman had studied, and twenty years after Schuman's damaging paper, he concluded:

Bear predation has little adverse effect on sockeye salmon production today. There is even less reason to believe that bear predation was responsible for the decline of salmon populations in the historical past, when the numbers of salmon were five times greater and bear populations, to the best of our knowledge, were not proportionately larger.

When Gard's study was published in 1971 I hoped it would end the bear-salmon controversy in Alaska forever. In 1994, however, the Alaska legislature passed the "intensive management law," which in effect directed the Alaska Board of Game to reduce some predator species, such as bears and wolves, in order to increase the numbers of big-game animals (such as moose) available for human harvest. So far this law has been applied only to limited areas. One wonders, however, if the same theory might be applied to the bear-salmon relationship. If so, the old controversy might again ignite.

We can only hope that the thousands of people who now flock to Alaska to view bears, and the thousands more who will follow, would thwart such a misguided effort.

FIGURE 43   *Various breeds of cattle were introduced to Kodiak Island, such as these Scottish Highland cattle.*

11

THE KODIAK BEAR–CATTLE WAR

In late April on Kodiak Island a group of *Hereford cattle grazed peacefully in a small meadow near Pasagshak Bay, unaware that a brown bear was in an alder patch only four hundred yards away. The cattle were feeding on new green shoots of grass and sedge protruding through last year's mat of dead vegetation that blanketed the drab landscape.*

A young male bear had left his den on a mountain slope above Hidden Basin about ten days before and immediately traveled down the snow-covered terrain to the seacoast in search of food. He ate anything available to satisfy his hunger. Occasionally the young boar consumed small green growths of cow parsnip and angelica or dug out the roots to add to his meager diet.

He followed the shoreline closely, searching for seals or other dead animals that might have washed up on the beach. Near Saltery Cove he came upon the remains of a dead cow. This was a new item on the menu, for he had never before smelled or tasted beef. The cow had been a victim of starvation during the harsh winter. Fox and eagles had devoured most of it, but he managed to find a few scraps of meat and chewed up the bones that contained a little marrow. He liked the taste of cow and, as the bear followed the coast, he constantly sniffed the air currents, hoping to find another one.

This morning as he grazed on small sprouts of green vegetation, the brownie was unaware that many cows were also feeding a few hundred yards below. A drizzling rain had washed away any fresh scent the cows might have left. The bear was feeding slowly downhill, occasionally lifting his head to sniff and scan the surroundings. The cattle were working uphill, gradually closing the gap between them.

Twenty minutes passed and, as the young male grazed between two alder patches, a gust of wind whipped the cows' scent to the bear. Alerted, he raised his head to look and sniff. He immediately associated the smell with the dead cow on the beach. Moving silently along the edge of the alders, his eyes and nose swept the landscape. The young boar padded along for a hundred yards, and then rose to his hind legs to improve his sight and sense of smell. Gazing intently, his small eyes detected the silhouette of several cattle looming through the foggy mists. The cow scent penetrated his nostrils

and saliva oozed from his lips in anticipation of a meal.

Oriented to the prey's location, the bear dropped to all four feet and crept forward through another alder patch. In a few minutes he was only fifty yards from the nearest cow. He waited patiently as she fed toward him, oblivious of the impending danger.

The distance between predator and prey gradually diminished; the lead cow was soon only sixty feet away, while three or four others were a few yards behind her. The bear crouched low, then exploded from the alders and charged swiftly toward her. She turned to run, but he was upon her in a few bounds, and with a mighty swat he raked his claws along her shoulders. The impact knocked the cow off her feet. His powerful jaws clamped down across her neck, breaking it instantly. In a moment the cow was dead. The bear would remain in the vicinity and gorge on the fresh meat for the next few days.

The historical conflict between cattle ranching and grizzlies in the western United States has been well documented and publicized. Ranchers considered the once-abundant grizzlies to be serious predators of cattle, and they ruthlessly hunted, trapped, and poisoned them. This led to the gradual extermination of the bears over most of their range. Few people, however, are aware that a similar conflict raged on Kodiak Island, for many years, resulting in the killing of hundreds of bears to enhance just a few small cattle operations.

Russians introduced a Siberian strain of cattle to Kodiak Island around 1794. According to H. W. Elliot, cattle populations never exceeded three hundred animals and were kept in the vicinity of Kodiak Village during the Russian era. About eighty to one hundred head were still present in 1900. In 1906, the U.S. Department of Agriculture established an Agricultural Experiment Station in Kalsin Bay near the town of Kodiak to explore the possibility of animal husbandry in Alaska. By 1907, employees had introduced a few Hereford and Galloway breeds in an attempt to upgrade and increase beef production.

The cattle population increased for a few years, but the 1912 Katmai eruption had a detrimental effect. Volcanic ash, eighteen inches deep, covered most of northeastern Kodiak Island where the cattle roamed. The ash buried and suppressed all vegetation that livestock utilized; most of the cattle, therefore, were butchered or removed from the island. Two years later vegetation began to return, and in July 1914 fifty head of cattle were reintroduced. The population remained low throughout the 1920s. Apparently the conflict with bears was of minor significance, probably because the livestock were kept near human habitation, closely tended, and not permitted to roam into major bear habitat. Hunters took brown bears commercially for their hides during this era before game regulations existed, and reportedly they were quite sparse around human settlements.

In the 1930s livestock numbers gradually increased. Three ranchers with herds of 54, 105, and 130 cattle moved their livestock into outlying areas where they were more vulnerable to bears. They reported huge losses to bears in 1937 and 1938.

Apparently this was the first time kills occurred in significant numbers, and the ranchers requested relief from the Secretary of Agriculture. Their request prompted the Alaska Game Commission to investigate these accusations in 1938 and 1939. The commissioners sent Hosea Sarber, a renowned bear hunter and employee of the Alaska Game Commission in Southeast Alaska, to Kodiak Island.

Sarber and several assistants killed eleven bears on or near the cattle ranches to reduce bear numbers. He reported that cattle losses attributed to bears by the ranchers were greatly exaggerated. Only five of the seventy-nine dead cows examined by Sarber appeared to have been killed by bears: the majority had succumbed to malnutrition, plant poisoning, falls, and other accidents and ailments.

Ranchers continued to make excessive and unfounded claims about bear kills throughout the bear-cattle conflict. Because of high feed costs, cattle grazed on open ranges throughout the year to cut down on supplemental feeding. During severe winters many starved and, when bears emerged from hibernation and wandered onto such kills, they readily fed on the dead animals. After the cows had been partially eaten by bears, no one could determine whether the cow had been killed by a bear or had succumbed to malnutrition prior to the bear's arrival. Perhaps it was only natural that ranchers tended to blame bears for their losses, and some deliberately exaggerated these losses to bring sympathy to their plight.

Most ranchers were hard workers and tended their stock as well as possible. The winter pastures along the tidal flats were usually fenced and livestock could be closely guarded. As the snows receded, however, the cattle moved into the uplands on the open range where alder and willow thickets provided habitat for bears. If a cow wandered into this mountain country with its dense vegetation and died or disappeared, ranchers assumed she had been killed by a bear. Whenever possible, ranchers hunted and shot bears on or near the pastures. They considered eliminating them to be part of their job. Thus was the stage set for fierce controversy between ranchers, who blamed most of the cattle deaths on bears, and conservationists, who felt bears were blamed unfairly.

As the killing of bears continued, conservation groups became concerned for their welfare and advocated establishing a brown bear refuge on Kodiak Island. Because of the marked difference of opinion between ranchers and conservationists, Secretary of the Interior Harold Ickes requested a special investigation, the conclusion of which recommended that the most suitable cattle range on Kodiak Island was a 480-square-mile area east and south of a line extending from Kupreanof Mountain to Kiliuda Bay. They estimated that the area was capable of supporting 3,800 head of cattle. This report was the basis for an executive order establishing the 1,954,611-acre Kodiak National Wildlife Refuge on August 19, 1941. A one-mile strip around the perimeter of the island was made available for homesteading, primarily to accommodate commercial fishing operations and homesites for fishermen living in the area. This loophole in the executive order would cause more problems and come to haunt conservationists in the future.

The bear-cattle conflict continued through the 1940s. During World War II, when up to sixty thousand troops were stationed in the area, the amount of human activity and hunting discouraged bears from using this part of the island. After the war, however, ranchers again claimed large losses to bears.

By the beginning of the 1950s the U.S. Bureau of Land Management (BLM) had issued six grazing leases on the northeastern portion of Kodiak Island and the cattle population had risen to 735. Most of these leases contained around twenty thousand acres regardless of how many cattle were present. In 1951 the Kodiak Stock Growers Association sent a representative to the Alaska Territorial Legislature requesting that it pass a resolution removing all protection of bears on Kodiak Island. On February 26, 1951, the Legislature passed House Joint Memorial No. 6, requesting a twelve-month open hunting season on bears without bag limits. A resolution requesting the same action by the Kodiak Chamber of Commerce soon followed. These actions antagonized national conservation and sportsmen's groups and pushed the bear-cattle controversy into a full-scale war. Ira Gabrielson wrote in *Audubon Magazine*, "If it comes to a choice between killing off the bears and trying to develop the optimistically estimated herd of 3,800 range cattle, it is my belief that this country ought to set aside the entire island to preserve the splendid Kodiak bears."

Bear-hunting guides joined the opposition to the open season. Guiding had become a lucrative business on Kodiak Island after World War II: guides were getting $1,000 per hunt and they feared that reduction of the bear population would jeopardize their profession. They lobbied the Alaska Game Commission not to implement such a liberal hunting season, and ultimately prevented the resolution from being enacted.

These conflicts and controversies prompted the U.S. Fish and Wildlife Service to dispatch Bob Burkholder to Kodiak in the summer of 1951 to initiate another investigation. Although ranchers had reported huge losses that year, Burkholder concluded that only ten cattle were taken by bears; he found numerous dead animals that appeared to have starved during the winter. The ranchers disputed his findings. Burkholder did remove five bears from the ranches in control operations.

The bear-cattle conflict was compounded in 1955 when the BLM, a sister agency of the Fish and Wildlife Service, issued two twenty-year grazing leases within the one-mile strip excluded from the Kodiak National Wildlife Refuge. The director of the BLM in Alaska and many of his subordinates sided with the cattle interests. They saw the loophole in the executive order creating the refuge and decided to start issuing leases on this crucial bear habitat. The Fish and Wildlife Service protested to no avail. Both agencies knew that ringing the perimeter of the refuge with cattle ranches could jeopardize the entire bear population on Kodiak Island. The new leases were a blow to conservationists who had fought so hard to establish the refuge for bears.

Politics and government policies forced a new compromise. I became manager of the Kodiak National Wildlife Refuge in 1955. Dave Spencer, Refuge Supervisor for Alaska's Wildlife Refuges, and I negotiated on behalf of the Fish and Wildlife Service; our opponent Gene Wunderlick, the BLM delegate, was a strong proponent of agriculture and livestock ranching in Alaska. During one of our field trips to Uganik Bay the sight of a small, experimental patch of oats planted by a rancher inspired him to envision great opportunities for agriculture there. BLM was threatening to issue grazing leases around the entire island, and Spencer and I were forced to compromise. The outcome was that in 1958 the Department of the Interior amended the executive order to exclude the Kupreanof and Shearwater peninsulas from the refuge; in exchange, the Fish and Wildlife Service gained complete jurisdiction of the one-mile strip. Additionally, the BLM canceled the Uganik Island lease, which had not

yet been stocked, and reduced the lease for Uganik Bay to accommodate the few sheep that had been placed there.

By 1956 the cattle population had reached 974 animals and ranchers continued to report exaggerated losses to bears. I remember one particularly fraudulent example. An absentee cattle rancher with a lease on Sitkalidak Island off the coast of Kodiak had stocked the island with more than a hundred head of cattle the previous year, and reported that bears were killing his cattle in great numbers. He wrote a letter to the secretary of the interior demanding that the government remove the bears from the island. The letter funneled down to the Fish and Wildlife Service in Alaska, and the regional director asked me to investigate the situation. When I arrived on Sitkalidak I contacted the resident ranch hand, who reported that no bears even existed on the island. He reported that the cattle were indeed dying, and he suspected disease. I spent two days surveying the area on foot and horseback and found only eight live cows among many dead ones. I reported my findings, and a veterinarian was next dispatched to the island. He discovered that the cattle had leptospirosis, an infectious disease, and he placed a quarantine on the island. I never heard from the rancher again.

Bear numbers in the ranching area at this time were actually quite low due to heavy hunting pressure by military personnel stationed at the U.S. Naval Station near Kodiak. The Predator Control Branch of the Fish and Wildlife Service did limited control work. Yet the conflict was kept alive through the late 1950s by ranchers and business leaders who felt that cattle ranching had a great economic future on Kodiak. At one point I gathered up several guides to attend the local Kodiak Chamber of Commerce meeting in an effort to dissuade the chamber from proposing additional bear-control measures.

In 1957 and 1958 the BLM issued two new grazing leases for Saltery Cove and Sharatin Bay. As a result, cattle were introduced into new areas and into good bear habitat. The lease owners immediately undertook bear control to prevent possible cattle losses. They were so secretive about their bear kills that I was never able to determine the total number of bears they took, but it was substantial.

On January 1, 1960, management of the fish and wildlife resources in the territory of Alaska came under the jurisdiction of the newly formed state of Alaska. In 1963, cattle kills by bears increased again—according to the ranchers, who sensed the possibility of more political clout with the state. They sent letters and telegrams to Alaska Governor William Egan, Senator Ernest Gruening, and State Commissioner of Fish and Game Walter Kirkness. The ranchers also requested from Senator Gruening a supply of 1080, the deadly poison used to exterminate coyotes and other predators in parts of the western United States.

The Alaska Department of Fish and Game responded by employing Dave Henley, a former rancher and World War II fighter pilot, to assist the ranchers in killing bears with the use of an aircraft. Henley mounted a .30 caliber M-1 semiautomatic rifle on top of a Piper Super Cub so that it would shoot above the propeller and be fired by an electronic device. Equipping the rifle with a Nydar optical sight, a scope used by the military in World War II, made it a very effective means of killing bears. Operating in as much secrecy as possible, Henley and his assistant, a volunteer, shot thirty-five bears from the air during the summer of 1963. The bears they killed were selected at random and often miles from any cattle.

Bear-hunting guides became aware of the operation and obtained photos of the plane with the mounted gun. Local newspapers and national magazines soon publicized the photos widely. *Outdoor Life* featured an article by Jim Rearden; the gun-equipped plane was depicted on the cover. National sportsmen's and conservation groups were incensed at the needless slaughter and demanded a stop to the practice. I believe that it was this episode that finally swung public opinion strongly in favor of bears and against the cattlemen who had waged war on them for so many years.

As a result of this outcry the Alaska Department of Fish and Game released a new policy statement on the Kodiak bear–cattle war in 1964 and initiated an intensive investigation of the bear-cattle conflict. The department assigned biologist Sterling Eide to the area. He reported that bears killed thirty-three cattle during the fourteen-month period from May 1, 1964 through June 30, 1965.

By this time cattle numbers on Kodiak had reached an all-time high of 1,350 animals, excluding spring calves, which were spread over eight grazing leases totaling 180,000 acres. The department sought to reduce bear numbers on the ranches by lengthening the bear-hunting season and encouraging hunting on or near the leases. Eide and his assistant shot nineteen bears in the area, hunters took four, and ranchers and Fish and Game personnel killed another fifteen in control operations. Most of the bears taken were adult males. Males tend to travel farther than females, and Eide speculated that bears were coming from outside the area. He proposed building a fence in an attempt to block bears from moving onto the ranches. For years, other investigators had also considered building a barrier across the mountains to block the ingress of bears. But studies had found such a project economically infeasible and impractical because the heavy winter snowfall would cover fences and permit bears to pass over the barriers in the early spring. This time one of the ranchers opposed the barrier for fear it would actually funnel bears onto his lease. Fish and Game never undertook the fencing project.

The Alaska Department of Fish and Game continued to do some control work on the ranching area through 1969, but in 1970 they changed their policy yet again and curtailed all bear-control work in the cattle area. Once the department got involved in the bear-cattle conflict, they saw the enormous problems that would ensue if ranching was allowed to expand into new areas of good bear habitat. They effectively blocked the state from issuing grazing leases on the Shearwater and Kupreanof peninsulas, the two areas BLM had insisted on excluding from the refuge in 1958 for the purpose of expanding the cattle industry.

Cattle ranching reached its peak in the 1960s. The tsunami from the 1964 earthquake swept over some of the lowlands and killed around 130 cattle. Several of the marginal cattle ranchers terminated their operations. The bear-cattle controversy also died down during the latter part of the 1960s and has not reignited in recent years. Some ranchers gave up cattle in favor of buffalo, which are not as vulnerable to bear predation as are cattle. In 1998 the Alaska Division of Agriculture reported approximately four hundred cattle and three hundred buffalo on Kodiak. Other ranchers now emphasize dude ranching.

In retrospect, the bear-cattle controversy was blown way out of proportion by a few vociferous ranchers and business leaders. Cattle ranching on the island was a marginal economic endeavor that never did have the enormous potential envisioned by its proponents. Bears were not the major cause for failure of the cattle industry, though in fairness to the ranchers, cattle killed by bears were a monetary loss to the owners and did make some contribution to their failure. Other problems included the difficulty and expense of transporting beef to markets, a lack of good slaughter facilities, the high cost of importing winter feed, the poor nutritional quality of Kodiak native grasses, winter starvation, and other natural causes of mortality.

In my opinion, cattle ranching should not have occurred on Kodiak Island since it was already inhabited by one of the densest bear populations in Alaska. Moreover, the value of the bears was recognized in 1941 when two-thirds of the island was set aside as a refuge. One must remember, however, that during this early period many residents of Alaska considered the brown bear to be a predator and a pest, and to them the only good bears were dead ones. In the present climate of growing environmental awareness and interest in large predators, the public is less likely to tolerate bear-control operations in order to enhance such a small cattle industry.

Today, large numbers of people travel to Kodiak Island just to see and photograph these grand animals, and the tourist industry associated with bear viewing far exceeds the economic value of the cattle industry. Most residents of the island now strongly support bear conservation. They are proud of the fact that they live next to one of the densest brown bear populations in the world. How times change!

FIGURE 44   *The Thumb Lake area of the Kodiak National Wildlife Refuge on Kodiak Island. Camp Island, in the foreground, was the headquarters for our early research.*

12

PIONEER BEAR-TRAPPING DAYS

IT HAD RAINED HEAVILY DURING THE NIGHT AND *torrents of water cascaded down the rocky slope of Halfway Creek as the three of us, clad in hip boots and raincoats, hiked along the edge of the stream. We had not gone far when I heard the brush crackling ahead. I yanked my hood back so I could hear more clearly. A loud drawn-out roar erupted far ahead—the sound of a bear in distress. Had we caught our first bear in the steel trap we had set a few days earlier?*

"Sure sounds like a mad bear to me," Earl muttered. We looked at each other nervously and readied our rifles and shotgun. We moved carefully forward toward the trap site. The trap was gone! A ragged, torn trail led upstream.

"Looks like we got one," I murmured to Earl and Ken. Up the trail several bushes lay ripped from the

ground, strewn about; the bark from several trees hung in shreds. Then we heard the chomping jaws and sniffs of an agitated bear. Had we caught a cub? Was the mother standing by to defend her offspring? Or did we have a single bear?

Earl and Ken looked at me with questioning eyes as if to say, "What do we do now?" I gestured toward the cottonwood trees; we climbed them. From my perch I could see a single bear, partially obscured in an alder thicket, struggling against the trap.

We slid down the trees and cautiously approached it. Earl set off a few firecrackers to make sure no other bears were around. We moved to within fifty feet of the brownie and watched it lunge widely, snapping limbs like matchsticks with its powerful jaws as it fought to free itself. The trap, however, had firmly caught the bear's front left foot. We judged that the young subadult would weigh around three hundred pounds. Small for a Kodiak bear, but I realized the job ahead would not be easy. Now, somehow, we had to rope the animal and get a bucket of ether over its head to anesthetize it long enough to enable us to gather the biological information we sought.

When I arrived on Kodiak Island in 1955, a few bear studies had been conducted by previous biologists. However, these were primarily defensive in nature: they were designed to contradict accusations that the bears on Kodiak were a major cause of the decline in salmon populations and a major obsta-cle to local cattle ranching. As refuge manager and a biologist, I realized that we needed more informa-tion on the life history and general biology of the Kodiak bear if we were to understand the animal, its behavior, and all the mysteries surrounding it.

I also knew that in order to gather this basic information I needed to perfect a method to live-trap, physically examine, and mark brown bears. No one in Alaska had ever done this. Biologists had devised methods to capture black bears in Michigan and New York, and in Yellowstone Park rangers caught nuisance grizzlies in culvert traps in order to move them. Modern drugs were still unknown; workers used ether to sedate animals.

That winter at our annual U.S. Fish and Wildlife Service meeting in Juneau I announced my intent to capture Kodiak bears. The audience reacted with loud laughter. I must admit that I too harbored a little skepticism about the whole project, but I was young, I had plenty of enthusiasm, and my inten-tions never wavered.

In 1956 I constructed two portable culvert traps with the help of personnel from the Kodiak Naval Base who were interested in the project. In the spring we flew the two culvert traps into Karluk Lake, a hundred miles from Kodiak in the heart of some of the best bear country on the island. We set one trap at Thumb River and the other near O'Malley River. Earl Fleming and Ken Durley, who assisted that summer, were seasonal employees. The traps were fourteen-gauge culvert sections, eight feet long by four feet wide, with a heavy steel gate on one end. When a bear grabbed bait attached to a wire trigger on the inside end of the trap, the raised gate would drop.

This operation seemed simple enough; we had some details to learn, however. Experimentation indicated that bacon was the most attractive bait,

FIGURE 45   *We used culvert traps to capture our first bears, but they proved inefficient. This one is set in the O'Malley River and Lake area near Karluk Lake, Kodiak National Wildlife Refuge.*

FIGURE 46   *The author displays a foot snare he used to capture bears on Camp Island, Karluk Lake, Kodiak National Wildlife Refuge.*

but we had difficulty enticing bears into the traps because of a plentiful supply of salmon and other food items. Bears or foxes occasionally stole baits without triggering the trap door until we fine-tuned the trigger setting.

One morning several weeks later, we checked a trap and found the gate down. I approached the trap and peeked into a small hole at the rear. Wham! A bear paw slapped against the hole I was peering into. I jumped back startled and thought, Now what? None of us had ever manhandled a bear before, and we were unsure of ourselves as we organized our equipment. We stuffed the holes of the trap with cloth to make it as airtight as possible; then we began spraying ether into openings with ordinary hand-pump fly sprayers. The trap, being far from airtight, allowed ether fumes to escape.

Unavoidably we inhaled some of the fumes; if we weren't careful, we would be unconscious before the bear was. After we pumped ether steadily for thirty minutes, the brownie lay down and seemed subdued. I poked it with a stick and got no reaction. Moving rapidly, we lifted the gate and removed the bear. It was small, probably less than three hundred pounds. I straddled the animal and placed over its head a bucket lined with ether-saturated cotton.

We needed several minutes to take measurements, examine the animal, and clamp colored tags in its ears for future sightings. As the ether dissipated, the bear attempted to stand upright before we had finished. I yelled for more ether as I struggled to remain astride the bear—cowboy-fashion—while at the same time holding the bucket over its muzzle. At last Ken managed to pour another cup

FIGURE 47   *The #150 double-spring steel trap with offset jaws (left side) was effective for capturing bears.*

of ether into the bucket. The additional ether did the trick, allowing us to finish installing the ear tags. By then, however, I was half-anesthetized and rather incoherent. "Led 'er go," I stammered.

"But we have to weigh the animal," Earl appealed.

"For-ged id," I replied, and let myself fall off the animal. The young bear, now loose and without its rider, staggered into the woods and disappeared.

Once the effects of the ether subsided, the three of us stood around talking excitedly. We had successfully captured and marked our first Kodiak bear! I was confident that we could start gathering important biological information. The research did not go quite that easily, however. With the plentiful food supply, bears remained unwilling to enter baited traps. During that summer we captured only three bears.

That winter I corresponded with black-bear biologists in several states. A few reported that they were now using steel traps or snares to capture black bears, then lassoing and hog-tying them. I reasoned that this technique could be applied to

brown bears, although I did have some apprehensions. What if we caught a huge bear that we could not handle? What if we caught a cub whose mother fought to defend it? I reasoned that the foot of a large bear probably would not fit into the small trap, and since cubs usually follow their mother, capturing a cub was unlikely. How wrong I was!

By the spring of 1958 I had acquired a dozen #150 double-spring traps with offset jaws. I hoped the offset jaws would allow space for the foot or toes without causing undue damage, and we wrapped the jaws with tape to dull the sharp edges. We attached a ten-foot chain with a three-pronged drag to each trap, hoping the drag would entangle in bushes and hold the animal.

We first tried bait sets, but these were not effective. Blind trail sets, however, proved very successful. We set traps in well-worn trails that led to salmon streams, concealing them with dirt, moss, and leaves. By placing a series of strategically placed sticks in the trails, we tricked the bears into stepping into the traps. No bait was needed.

The first few bears we captured were young subadults in the 200- to 350-pound range. We managed to lasso these animals, tie them down on their backs, and anesthetize them by placing a bucket with ether over their heads. We barely avoided being bitten on two occasions, but we did successfully process several bears, as well as gain confidence and valuable experience.

Then the unexpected happened. One morning as we approached a trail set on Salmon Creek, the loud bawl of a yearling cub broke the silence. We looked at each other in alarm; we were sure it was caught in a trap. What if the mother were there to meet us? We were still a hundred yards away. I slipped my rifle from my shoulder, jacked a shell into the chamber, and peered into the woods. I spotted a cub struggling in the trap as the sow and another cub milled around. I could tell the sow was agitated. She was slobbering, snapping her jaws, and constantly changing direction, on guard for any intruder. "Jiminy crickets!" I hissed. "What are we going to do now?"

Whispering to each other, we tried to formulate our next move. This silent approach, we later found, was the wrong method. Noise, *a lot* of noise, was the best answer to quell an angry, excited sow.

Suddenly she spotted us and came running at full speed. We did not have time to think, only react. Raising the rifle, I fired into a small stream directly in front of her, some forty yards away. I did not wait to see her response, but whirled and ran for a cottonwood tree. Earl and Ken were already climbing nearby trees. I grabbed for a branch, trying to propel myself up, but my feet repeatedly slid along the bark without making any upward progress. Any second I expected to feel her bite into my leg. An eternity passed, and I was still on the ground! I peeked around the tree and with enormous relief saw the sow running back to the trapped cub. Apparently the sound of the shot and the spray of water when the bullet hit the stream had frightened her. She could have easily caught me. Needless to say, we were shaken.

We fired more shots and shouted. The distraught mother snorted and slobbered profusely. We kept up the noise and harassment; after a few minutes she ran with her other yearling cub into the woods. To keep her going, Earl set off a few firecrackers that he had been carrying for just such an encounter.

While one of us stood guard with the rifle, the other two subdued the cub, took the biological data, tagged both ears, and released the animal. The adrenaline was still running high as we left the scene. We had now successfully captured and processed several bears and scared away one angry sow. We were elated! Luck and grit played a big part in our first successful efforts, but more adventures awaited us.

A few days later we followed the drag marks of another trap around some alder patches. When we came upon the bear, she was in a violent mood, lurching widely from side to side and attempting to tear free. I climbed up on a nearby fallen tree to get a better look. I was horrified, for we had caught a huge sow. She probably weighed six hundred pounds. Mad as a hornet, she growled and bit off several limbs as we watched in awe. I hoped the trap would hold as she lunged at us. I did not know about the others, but I was scared.

We tried to get a rope over her head several times, but each time she bit it in two as if it were a small thread. We then slipped a steel cable over her neck and attempted to hold her. Earl kept yelling, "Hang on!" And I yelled back, "Brace your feet!" But she jerked us around as if we were only minor annoyances, and finally succeeded in getting the cable off. Every time we threw a rope, she leaped toward us. That bear was one furious animal and I could not blame her. We backed off to regroup, and stood there for a few moments watching her powerful movements. My heart pounded wildly as my mind raced. Finally I said, "Guys, this one is too big to handle. We have to release her."

"How are you going to do that?" Earl asked, discouraged.

"I don't know," I answered in a subdued tone, "but we've got to do something."

We had a huge bear caught in a trap by her hind foot, could not hog-tie it, and had no idea how to release it. After considerable discussion we decided that, with the rifle, I would attempt to hit the main bolt that held the trap together, hoping it would

FIGURE 48   *The author measuring the hind foot of a large bear near Karluk Lake, Kodiak National Wildlife Refuge.*

By 1958 researchers had developed some new drugs that were being used on black bears. We gathered as much information on them as possible, and that winter we experimented with a captive bear in Anchorage. Al Erickson, a new biologist for the Alaska Territorial Fish and Game Department, had used the drugs succinylcholine and phenobarbital sodium on black bears and was able to give us some valuable advice.

Succinylcholine causes animals to lose muscle control. It takes effect quickly—within two minutes or so—but lasts a maximum of only ten minutes. We reasoned that we could trap an animal and then, while someone attracted its attention in front, another could stab the rear leg muscle from behind with a syringe fastened to the end of a twelve-foot aluminum pole. Once the bear was subdued, we could inject it with phenobarbital sodium and put it to sleep. The first drug often wears off before the second takes effect, so we learned how to rope all four legs and tie the animal spread-eagled on its back to keep it immobilized.

We had acquired more traps and a newly invented foot snare by the following summer. When a bear stepped inside the snare loop, a steel spring fired a steel cable upward around its foot. A drag was attached to the cable, which worked the same as the conventional trap chain. We had also obtained a supply of succinylcholine and phenobarbital sodium and the materials needed to deliver them.

Things went smoothly in 1959. The drugs took effect when properly administered and our delivery system seemed practical. Jabbing a bear in the rear leg muscle, however, was difficult when it was thrashing about. Our trapping and snaring techniques gradually improved, and trail sets were successful in taking bears on a regular basis. We captured, processed, and released thirty bears that summer. I was pleased that

break and release the jaws. Ken and Earl got in front to attract her attention. I slipped about thirty feet behind the bear, took aim, and fired. The trap fell away from her foot. I was dumbfounded, for I had no confidence that the bullet would pierce the bolt, let alone that I could hit such a small target. Ken and Earl scattered as she galloped off into the woods.

We were relieved to see her go. We had overcome another dilemma but had a ruined trap. The bullet had driven the bolt through the trap hinge. Of eight bears captured with traps that summer, the old sow was the only one that we could not handle.

we had been able to establish a successful method of capturing brown bears at last.

During the next five years we captured and processed around two hundred bears, some of which were recaptures. We learned a lot about brown bear behavior and handling procedures, as well as things to avoid. The biological data began to accumulate, and the bear work became almost routine.

Over the years, the methods we developed were increasingly safe and humane. Of the two hundred bears we processed, we lost just three. Two of these were killed in a trap by other bears before we arrived, and a third was accidentally overdosed with drugs. We never had to kill an animal in self-defense; we deterred a number of charges by shouting or firing in front of the agitated bear or by scaring it away with "shellcrackers," firecrackers placed inside a twelve-gauge shotgun shell with a range of one hundred yards or so. And as for the humans involved, except for a few bruises and scratches, we came through unscathed.

In retrospect, our early methods of trapping and snaring bears had to be very stressful to the animals. Once a bear had a foot caught in a device, it often fought for hours trying to get loose. True, some animals gave up fighting, lay down, and fell asleep until we arrived, but most continued to fight the trap or snare.

The females with cubs were probably the most traumatized when one of their captured cubs bawled loudly, struggling to free itself. The mother often rushed around in circles, huffing and snorting. At times the trapped cubs had been held for several hours before we arrived. Our further handling of the cub no doubt increased the distress the family was already under; we fired guns and shouted, trying to get the loose animals to back off so we could process and release it. In spite of

FIGURE 49   *Dick Hensel weighing one of the first bears we captured and sedated in the Karluk Lake area, Kodiak National Wildlife Refuge.*

the trauma our efforts caused, the female nearly always returned to reclaim her cub very soon after we left. In some cases we noted that, after this experience, bear families were more wary of humans than before. During this early pioneer work, we used the least disturbing methods we knew of to capture the animals. We thought the stress we caused was worth the valuable biological information we were getting, particularly because the data has been used to correct the kinds of misconceptions about bears that ignited the bear-cattle and bear-salmon wars.

I had very little contact with bears after I left Kodiak in 1963. During the next eleven years I worked with moose, sheep, caribou, and other species. In 1974 the National Park Service offered me a field biologist position that would include brown bear research in Katmai National Monument; I jumped at the opportunity.

Scientists had improved or invented many biological aids since I had last captured Kodiak bears, and the transition was not unlike going from horse and buggy to modern cars. Biologists now used radio collars on many wildlife species, permitting the rapid accumulation of information that had previously taken years to acquire. New, improved Cap-chur guns and new drugs were available, and efficiently darting animals from helicopters became routine. All of these improvements meant less stress for bears and humans alike.

In the mid-1970s the National Park Service needed more biological information on the brown bears at Brooks River, where bears were attracting tourists. The superintendent wanted the data to be gathered discreetly, with as little harassment as possible, so I decided to radio-collar bears by stalking them on foot and using dart guns to deliver the anesthesia. This method needed to be done in the late fall after the tourists had left Brooks and while the bears were still concentrated in the area.

I had no problem getting support from Alaska Department of Fish and Game personnel. Seasonal park rangers and my assistant Martin Grosnick helped with the project. Stalking bears on foot was challenging and adventurous, and fantastic fall trout fishing in the Brooks River during our free time was a bonus.

We usually worked in teams of two or three. One person carried the dart gun, while another helped with drugs, darts, and other equipment. One of us always carried a twelve-gauge shotgun loaded with slugs or buckshot for safety purposes. We rarely needed shellcrackers on this project since we were interested only in capturing adult animals; we never attempted to take cubs or yearlings, thus avoiding the parental aggressiveness we faced at Kodiak.

Each morning just before dawn we left the cabin eager and excited, anticipating the unknown. We walked to the edge of Naknek Lake to scan the beach for bears. If none were present we followed bear trails along Brooks River in the predawn semi-darkness, hoping not to encounter a bear unexpectedly in the brushy habitat.

We checked likely riffles and pools as we picked our way along the river edges where bears might be feeding. When we sighted a suitable animal, the stalk began. If one was moving in our direction, we sought out a hiding spot and waited for the bear to close the distance between us.

We had to use extreme caution, as a bear's senses of sight, hearing, and smell are very keen. We always approached the animal from upwind. Accidentally stepping on a stick could end our stalk in failure. We had to get within eighty feet or less to deliver the dart. This was no easy feat and all our outdoor skills were required to outfox the bear. Once close enough to estimate the size of the bear, we loaded the dart with Sernylan, the drug we used at the time. Guessing the weight of the bear with enough accuracy to load the correct dosage was an art; an underdose would fail to fully anesthetize the animal and an overdose could kill it.

All encounters followed a similar procedure. As the bear got closer, the tension heightened. Would it come within range, or would the animal detect us at the last moment with its keen nostrils and bolt out of sight? We got only one shot, and we had to decide when the bear was close enough to attempt it. If the animal stopped for a while and we had to wait in silence, the tension mounted. Should we chance a long shot and possibly miss, or would we get a better opportunity? Sometimes, when success appeared imminent, the bear would suddenly change direction and disappear.

One episode was typical. The bear had moved forward again and stood less than eighty feet away. It was time. My mind ran through a calming sequence: Make sure the gun sight is on the shoulder or rear leg muscle, be calm, touch the trigger. Thwack! The dart hit home. I hoped the barbed needle would hold long enough to deliver the drug.

We ran for vantage points that provided a good view of the direction in which the animal was headed. Most of the Brooks River area is covered with dense stands of willow, alders, spruce, and birch; the bear could disappear in a hurry and might be difficult to find. The drug usually took effect in a couple of minutes, slowing the bear to a walk, and then causing it to fall or to lie down on the ground and remain immobilized for an hour or two. In the old days at Kodiak a second drug had had to be injected to put the animal to sleep; this newer method was a big improvement.

We waited about five minutes after darting the animal before starting the search. With help from seasonal rangers, we conducted a systematic hunt for the bear by spreading about a hundred feet apart and hiking through the woods in the direction the bear had taken. When one of the team discovered the brownie, a yell resounded along the line of searchers: "We found the bear!" From that point, our work became routine.

Processing a bear involved measuring and weighing, taking blood and hair samples, extracting a residual premolar tooth for purposes of determining the animal's age, inserting ear tags, and applying a radio collar. This normally required about thirty minutes. After we finished, we always waited for the bear to recover or checked the site later to make sure that it had left the area.

After we had darted a few bears successfully, we gained confidence, but found that each encounter had its own characteristics. Every bear reacted differently; every stalk became an adventure, sometimes a frightening one. We had many close encounters at Katmai, just as we had at Kodiak, but no one was ever injured.

We captured far fewer bears at Katmai than we had at Kodiak. By tracking the animals with radio collars, we were able to glean much more information on movements and other life history data from a few animals than we had accumulated from the numerous bears we marked with ear tags and colored markers at Kodiak. Moreover, stalking and darting bears was far less traumatic to the animal than the trap or snare methods used at Kodiak. Usually the animal was unaware of our presence until the dart hit it. The drug took effect within two minutes; the bear remained anesthetized for two hours or so. During this period we placed a radio collar on the animal and gathered the needed biological information. The collar is no doubt irritating to the bear for a few days, but the animal gets used to it.

At present, biologists dart wild animals, including brown bears, from helicopters. Frequently they must chase them for several hundred yards before making a successful hit. Capturing and anesthetizing any wild animal without causing some stress is nearly impossible; the data obtained, however, is often helpful in perpetuating the species.

Looking back on my experiences, I am glad I had the opportunity to capture bears without modern technology. But I am not sure that I would want to repeat it.

FIGURE 50   *Being charged by a bear is a terrifying experience.*

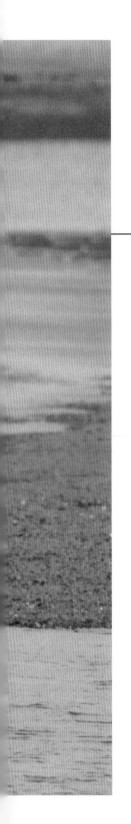

13

CHARGES AND COUNTERCHARGES

BILL COOPER WAS A LONER. HE PREFERRED BEING BY *himself when hiking or camping. One day a small tour boat deposited him on the end of a sloping ridge in the middle of Glacier Bay in Southeast Alaska.*

Tossing his heavy pack on his back, Cooper began hiking up the ridge. As he gained altitude, new vistas unfolded before him. High, snow-covered mountains towered in the skies on each side of the ridge, their peaks disappearing into the clouds above. Here and there glaciers flowed out of the mountains to the seas and discarded their ancient icy remains until the bay was filled with shiny icebergs. This wild, primordial scene seemed to go on forever.

Cooper took his time ascending the ridge, enjoying the grandeur of the wild country. After five hours of hiking he found an ideal campsite on a narrow ledge that fell steeply to the sea a thousand feet below. From this spot he had a 360-degree view of the world around him. He did not expect to see any other hikers; it was a lonely place that befitted a lonely man.

The camper pitched his orange tent and laid out his sleeping bag. Near his tent, he set down his pack, which was filled with food. He decided to take a short hike, check out the surroundings, and shoot a few photographs with the small camera he carried. As he walked away from camp, he was unaware that a visitor was approaching from the opposite direction—a brown bear.

The bear had left the coastal rain forest the week before and followed a large glacial draw into the bleak, rugged country that was far removed from its usual home range. It continued inland, crossing several moraines and valleys that contained little vegetation. The bear ambled through the empty country, occasionally nipping the tops of a few sparse sedges and horsetail. Each night it bedded down in a ravine, and each day it wandered over countless ridges. Perhaps it would find a new range filled with food; its hunger grew as it continued the lonely trek.

A few minutes after Cooper left his camp, the bear topped a ridge, spotted the orange tent, and made a cautious approach. From fifty yards or so it sniffed the air and caught the scent of food. That welcome smell drew it straight for the tent and, in a few minutes, the bear had its nose in Cooper's pack, ripping open packages of dried food, candy

bars, dry milk, and rice. It was strange food to the bear, but it helped satisfy the hunger that gnawed at its empty stomach.

In the meantime Cooper had taken his circular hike, shooting a few scenic photos. As he approached the camp, he spotted the bear. The hiker took a photo of the bear, and then began to yell and scream, hoping to drive it off his supplies. The bear paid no heed and continued to ransack the pack and the tent, searching for more food. Cooper picked up a rock, ran closer, and flung it at the bear. The lucky throw hit the marauder in the ribs with a thunk, but instead of running, the brownie turned on Cooper, not willing to share the food with the intruder. As the bear made a charging rush, Cooper turned to run. It was a fatal decision. Cooper died as he had lived, alone in the wild and lonely land.

Bear maulings are extremely rare. When one does happen, the event becomes news throughout the country. Perhaps the ancient, primitive struggle of man and beast arouses public interest. Outdoor magazines and even family publications such as *Reader's Digest* often carry vivid accounts of people being mauled by bears in the wilderness. Every gory detail is described, as if Jack the Ripper had been turned loose.

Because of such accounts, many people are extremely apprehensive about traveling through bear country. Yet statistics indicate that your chances of getting injured or killed in a vehicle on the nation's highways are at least fifty times greater than in bear country.

It is important to remember that bears are individuals. Their temperaments and behaviors vary, and each individual may react differently in a given situation. Brown bears tend to be curious and frequently want to investigate a person walking through their territory. I have often watched bears become aware of my presence, then stand on their hind legs, peering intently for a moment. If they are still not sure about me, they may come closer, then stand up for another look before deciding to flee or ignore me. Sometimes they circle downwind to catch my scent before making a decision to run. This behavior is typical of bears that have encountered few people.

I have camped in bear country for many years and have never had any serious bear problems. However, I did experience one alarming incident. I was camped alone on a ledge above Canyon Creek on Kodiak Island. During the middle of the night I became aware that I had company. A bear was quietly circling my tent, making woofing sounds. I was sure it was going to try to enter, so I sat with my rifle in my lap. The night was extremely still, but occasionally I could hear a twig snap and the sound of breathing. I yelled loudly a few times, but the bear continued to circle, seemingly unafraid. After about thirty minutes, it finally left. I was never sure whether the bear was just curious or had detected food odors.

Even if you are careful, someone who used your campsite before you may have been irresponsible with food. If a bear does arrive and is obviously looking for food, it is best to pick up your pack and move on. It does not pay to take chances with a bear that associates campers with an easy meal. One careless person can endanger subsequent visitors.

Bears can be dangerous; bear attacks can be fatal. But the odds that you will become a victim are very, very remote. I tell my friends that traveling through bear country is similar to walking through a city. If you take precautions and follow the rules, you will not have any problems. If you are careless in traffic or enter a dangerous, dark alley, you may end up in trouble. The following precautions should be taken by anyone traveling through bear country:

1. Carry all food double-wrapped in plastic bags to keep odors to a minimum. Nearly all parks now provide bear-resistant food containers (BRFCs) that campers are required to use.

2. Pick your campsite carefully. Do not camp near bear trails or food sources such as a stream filled with spawning salmon.

3. If possible, pick a site that has tall trees in which you can hang your food out of a bear's reach. I always carry a few long ropes that can be tossed over a limb to hoist the food sacks high in the air. If no trees are available, store your food on a rocky ledge or other spot that bears rarely frequent. Most important, keep the food away from the tent.

4. Keep dishes clean. Dishwater and other wastes should be dumped well away from the camp.

5. Place all garbage in plastic bags and carry it out.

Brown bears may react violently if they feel threatened or cornered. The following situations will typically make a bear feel threatened, and should be avoided at all costs:

FIGURE 51   *These fishermen in Brooks River left a pack with food on a small islet, which a bear discovered. This is a sure method of getting in bear trouble.*

1. Getting too close to a sow with cubs. A mother is naturally protective of her offspring; she feels crowded if something comes between her and her cubs. She may feel threatened and react quickly to encourage you to leave. Normally, if a sow with young sees you in time, she gathers up the cubs and flees the area.

2. Getting too close to a breeding pair. During the breeding season when males and females are paired the boar is very protective of his mate. The male may treat you like another boar competing for his mate. His message is: "Stay away, I'm a jealous lover!"

3. Getting too close to a bear guarding its food cache. When bears kill a large animal such as a moose or caribou, they may feed on it for several days and remain in the vicinity of the carcass to defend it from intruders (see chapter 7). People have been attacked when they stumble accidentally onto a bear's food cache. Be vigilant for signs of a bear kill, including concentrated bear tracks, disturbed vegetation, and groups of ravens or eagles descending into or perched in trees. Take a wide detour around these features.

4. Surprising a bear at close range. A bear that is startled by your presence at close quarters may react suddenly and violently before leaving the scene. Bears are much like some people who lash out in all directions before running if they think an attack is imminent.

CHAPTER THIRTEEN

Unfortunately, a quick slap of a bear's paw or nip of its teeth can do considerable damage to a human. The same reaction to another bear would rarely draw blood. To avoid such an encounter, hikers should make plenty of noise when walking through brushy habitat. Walking downwind or detouring around dense vegetation is the wisest choice, even if it means taking a longer route.

5. Coming into contact with a bear that has learned to associate humans with food. The most dangerous bear of all is one that has lost all fear of humans and associates them with a potential source of food. Usually this type of behavior develops around camps or small settlements that do not have adequate garbage disposal facilities. Landfills without bear-proof fencing or incinerators often attract bears from long distances. Once a bear is conditioned to human food, it can become a real pest. It is difficult to break a bear of its habits, and preventing this association from ever happening is the best solution.

A number of years ago while I was working for the National Park Service, I was sent to Glacier Bay National Park to investigate the circumstances in which a brown bear had killed a camper in a remote part of the park. I arrived at the lodge and met with a friend to discuss the catastrophe. While we were talking, an employee rushed into the room and blurted, "I'm sorry to bother you, but there is a bear in my office!" We went to investigate and, sure enough, we found a black bear in her office with its head in a wastepaper basket scrounging for food. We eventually chased the bear out of the building and into the nearby woods.

Later that evening, when I returned to my room at the lodge, I saw a black bear walking across the deck. The next day I inspected the local garbage dump, which was only two miles away, and found it unfenced. When I slammed shut my car door, seven bears came sauntering out of the woods, anticipating the garbage truck with a fresh load of refuse. The driver of the garbage truck later informed me that the bears sometimes jumped into the vehicle before it was unloaded. I was appalled: this substandard garbage facility, which had taught bears to associate humans with food, was obviously the underlying reason that bears had begun to wander into the lodge to look for food. The following year the Park Service fenced the dump, greatly reducing the bear problem.

When bears become a "problem," it is often because of a situation created by humans, rather than because of anything innate in a bear's personality. Being able to recognize a problem bear, identify the cause of its stress, and knowing how to deal with it is very important. Animals that feel threatened or agitated give definite physical and audible warnings. A nervous, agitated bear can be very dangerous.

Many times, stressed bears make false charges. They run toward you full-bore, then stop, hoping to scare you away. They are saying, "Get out of here or I'll smack you." It works with me—being charged by a bear is a terrifying experience, and an agitated bear is best left alone.

Curious bears, or ones that want to test you, can also become dangerous. This is particularly true of juveniles or cubs that approach you. In this case, a short rush toward the cub is often wise, yelling and stomping your feet or throwing a stick. It will teach young bears to respect humans and let them know that you will not tolerate any closer contact.

FIGURE 52   *When hiking, be aware of bear signs, including trails. Do not camp near bear trails and other heavily used bear areas.*

During my years of capturing bears for study, I was charged a number of times by angry, excited mothers whose cubs were caught in a trap or snare. These were abnormal situations, but they did give me an opportunity to observe the behavior of the sows under extreme stress. Usually the behavioral sequence involved long stares in our direction when we first arrived, followed by woofing, popping jaws, and often foaming saliva oozing from their mouths. They then retreated, held their ground, or moved toward us. In some cases they launched into a full running charge. Our response was to yell, wave our arms, and sometimes discharge a firearm or lob a shellcracker several feet in front of them. They always broke off the charge to return to their cub, continuing to woof and stomp around. Eventually, with constant harassment, they left.

One fall when I was doing research at Brooks River, a small female with two yearling cubs arrived in camp. She was an extremely nervous and feisty little sow. If we got too close to her and her cubs, she exploded toward us in a fast charge and did not break it off until she was within fifteen or twenty feet. Then she would huff, chomp her teeth, and stomp her feet a few times before turning and walking away. Her yearlings frequently ran by her side or followed behind her when she initiated the charge. Her method was an effective way of putting fear into anyone who encountered her explosive mood. Apparently that was her intention. For obvious reasons we dubbed her Scary.

The tourist season had ended, fortunately, and only a few experienced park personnel were in camp. Even so we were caught in the open a number of times and had to submit to her scary tactics. Ranger Rollie Ostermick once spent an hour in a tree waiting for her to leave. A lot of yelling usually meant someone was receiving her attention. I was her intended victim two or three times, but each time I was near a cabin and managed to escape inside.

We finally decided to radio-collar her, but it took several days of effort before I outwitted Scary and shot a dart into her hindquarters. Once she was collared, I stepped outside of the cabin each morning with my receiver and antenna to record her approximate location. That way we managed to avoid the testy sow.

If you do encounter a bear that is obviously agitated and about to charge, you should take several actions:

1. Face the bear and start waving your arms while talking loudly.

2. If you have a coat, raise it over your head to look as big as possible. A better tactic is to carry a large lightweight garbage bag in your rear pocket. If a bear approaches, snap it over your head. In addition to making you look big, the snapping bag makes a lot of noise.

3. If you are with a group of people, remain close together.

4. If the bear continues to act in a threatening manner, make more noise, yell loudly, pound metal cans, blow whistles or sound an air horn, and continue to wave your arms.

5. Most bear experts would advise you to hold your ground; I prefer to back off a little bit, *but very slowly*, to give the bear more room. If your retreat causes the bear to advance again, stop and hold your ground.

6. *Never, never turn and run*. Running from a bear is the worst possible reaction. It typically

incites the bear to chase after you, triggering an instinctive predator/prey response.

7. If the bear continues to make aggressive moves toward you, throw rocks or sticks toward the bear. If you have a gun, fire a shot into the air or into the ground in front of the bear.

8. Only in dire circumstances—a full charge in close quarters—should you attempt to shoot a bear. *Instantly killing a charging bear with one shot is almost impossible.* An enraged, wounded bear is the worst predicament imaginable.

Bears are much less likely to attack groups of people than an individual or a couple. They seem to respect numbers and size. I have often considered attaching a large balloon to my hat that could be instantly inflated if a bear problem developed. Suddenly looking twice your height or size should be a great deterrent to a bear. I will leave that invention for someone else to develop.

Sometimes a bear that is advancing toward you is unaware of your presence. In this situation, the ideal response is to move away and give it room to pass. If you cannot avoid the approaching bear and it is obviously going to get too close, clap your hands or yell to make sure it knows you are there. It is better to surprise it at a distance than when it is almost upon you.

A number of mechanical devices are available to deter bear aggression. The most obvious is a firearm. Should you carry one, or not? That depends in part upon your experience with such weapons and how you feel about having one. If you are not well trained in the use of guns, I would not recommend carrying one. In some areas, such as in many national parks, you are not permitted to carry a firearm. During my bear-trapping years and throughout most of my career, I carried either a rifle or a shotgun. A twelve-gauge shotgun with slugs or double-00 buckshot is effective at close range. I used to carry shellcrackers in the shotgun as a loud scaring device, with slugs as backup (see chapter 12).

In the past few years, I have quit carrying a gun; instead I pack a can of pepper spray and a small flare gun. The gun makes a loud pop when it goes off and the flare can be bounced toward the bear. It should not be used, however, around dry vegetation that could ignite a fire. Pepper spray is an effective deterrent in most instances. It does have drawbacks: it can be used only at extremely close range, and the bear must be downwind from you or else the contents will blow back in your face.

I have used pepper spray only twice. The first time I was with some English photographers on the Katmai Coast when we encountered a yearling cub with its mother. The sow was a relatively tolerant bear and gave us no problems, but the yearling became curious and decided to test us. It kept advancing in spite of our shouting and stomping. It would stop for a few moments, and then come toward us again. I was not too concerned with the cub, but I was afraid the mother might become alarmed and intervene if the cub got too close. I sent my companions back to our small boat, then turned with the spray can to face my young adversary.

As the yearling topped a bank about thirty-five feet away, I gave it a shot of spray. I knew this was a bit far, but I thought the wind would carry the contents to the young intruder. Unfortunately, it settled in the grass just short of the bear's nose. Just then the mother topped the rise and the pair sniffed the stuff. They rolled around in it like a dog rolls in fresh horse dung. It was not quite the response I had hoped for, but it did give me time to get to the boat.

The second incident was similar. We were photographing two juveniles who tested us on several occasions. They made short bluff charges, not stopping until they were within twenty feet in spite of our yelling and arm waving. I grabbed a can of pepper spray and gave them a shot as they again started a charge from thirty-five feet. Though the contents reached the bears, it had dissipated by the time it got there, settling on the ground around them. Again the reaction of the bears was to roll around in the smelly stuff.

I have never had the opportunity to use the pepper spray at close range, but a number of people have, with desirable results. I do recommend carrying it for use in close quarters. It should be especially effective if a bear is trying to get into your tent.

In his book *Bear Attacks: Their Causes and Avoidance*, Stephen Herrero documents instances of grizzly and black bear attacks in Canada and elsewhere. Much of the information is applicable to the coastal brown bear and well worth reading. I also recommend *Living in Harmony with Bears*, published by the National Audubon Society. It is a concise booklet that gives excellent advice for traveling through bear country.

FIGURE 53   *Two photographers in Hallo Bay, Katmai National Park, use long telephoto lenses to keep a safe distance from the bears.*

14

VISITING BEAR COUNTRY

THE FEMALE BROWN BEAR WHITE-CLAW HAD SPENT *many years near Brooks River. She plodded along a familiar trail through grassy meadows and dense patches of willow. Near Brooks River Falls, the old female stepped out of the bushes and into the river to scan her surroundings. Two bears sat on top of the falls, waiting to catch a leaping red salmon, while a couple of large, dark-colored males and a small juvenile stood in the pool below the cascade, hoping for a meal.*

White-Claw waded to the edge of the river just above the falls and staked out a fishing spot as the water swirled around her legs. She occasionally turned her head to look upstream to make sure no other bears approached her from behind. A few minutes later the two males got into a sparring match, their roars resonating above the noise of the turbulent waters.

Salmon leaped steadily in their attempts to clear the precipice. Occasionally one landed atop the barrier and powered its way through the fast water toward the spawning grounds. White-Claw stood patiently at the top of the falls for about five minutes before a red salmon leaped high in the air near her left front paw. She lunged and caught the salmon in midair. The large fish struggled to free itself, but the bear held it firmly in her clenched teeth, then turned to wade across the river. She was oblivious to the snapping camera shutters and the oohs and aahs of the thirty-three bear watchers who stood on the viewing platform only 120 feet away.

Successful travelers take time to prepare themselves for trips to other countries and cultures. They learn something about the customs, proper dress, and rules of etiquette of the land they are touring. They honor the culture they are visiting and, by showing courtesy, gain the respect of their hosts.

Visitors to wilderness areas have similar obligations. Our very presence there introduces a new factor into the ecosystem and we should be mindful of the impacts we are having on the area and its wildlife. It is vital for us to be aware that, while we want to be "up close and personal" for our own benefit and enjoyment, we must maintain a comfort zone for the wild animals so that they are able to continue their daily activities.

Watching and photographing bears has become extremely popular in the last few decades. Bear country is getting more and more crowded. As visitors, our goal should be to disturb the animals as little as possible. If you take the right precautions while watching or photographing brown bears, your chances of being injured are extremely low.

Some bear-watching camps, such as Brooks in Katmai National Park and McNeil River Sanctuary, have operated very successfully in bear country with a minimum of people-bear conflicts. The facilities at Brooks include a lodge with adjoining cabins and a campground with tent sites. In addition, small tour groups fly in for one-day bear viewing. Sometimes several hundred people are in the area on a given day. To my knowledge only two people have been injured by bears there in more than thirty years of operation: a visitor was bitten in the buttocks and a ranger was clawed in the hand.

The National Park Service has taken a number of steps at Brooks to avoid bear problems and promote harmony between the people and the animals:

1. Rangers give each visitor a brief orientation on bears.

2. All garbage is removed from camp each day and hauled to a bear-proof dump five miles away.

3. Campers are required to store all food in hard-sided sheds surrounded by an electric fence.

4. Fishermen must place their catches in large plastic bags to avoid odors and clean their fish in a special house constructed for this purpose. Fish wastes are ground and flushed into an underground sewage system.

5. Several elevated viewing platforms overlooking Brooks Falls and the river are available for visitors while they are watching bears.

FIGURE 54   *Elevated platforms available in some areas provide a safe place to view and photograph bears. These viewers are at Brooks Falls at Brooks Camp, Naknek Lake, Katmai National Park.*

6.   Everyone is warned to keep fifty yards from single bears and one hundred yards from all family groups when not on the platforms.

7.   Park Service rangers discourage bears from coming near the lodge, but allow them to use the beach along Naknek Lake as a travel corridor.

Despite all these preventative measures, a few problems have occurred. The Brooks River is a popular fishing stream and occasionally, when fishermen are playing trout or salmon in shallow waters, bears are attracted to the wriggling fish. Anglers sometimes cut the line to release their catch, but often they will drop their gear and run. After a few such experiences, some bears learn to follow fishermen for an easy meal. During my latter seasons at

Brooks, a bear named Sister became very adept at taking fish from fishermen. Rangers tried to break her of the habit, but failed. She was eventually removed from the area. Considering the human-bear interactions that occur daily at Brooks, the rarity of injuries there is amazing.

McNeil Sanctuary also has a long safety record. The Alaska Department of Fish and Game has rigid requirements in camping areas. Personnel experienced in bear behavior closely supervise all visitors and fly all garbage to Homer. The number of people allowed at McNeil Falls is far lower than the number permitted at Brooks. All visitors are required to use the same site near the falls to watch bears. This keeps bear disturbance at a minimum.

These are examples of camps that have managed people and bears extremely well. Unfortunately,

FIGURE 55   *The author photographing bears at Hallo Bay in Katmai National Park.*

incidents do occur in bear country where residents do not behave responsibly—for example, when they have not properly disposed of garbage. A few unethical owners of camps or lodges feed bears to attract them. This is illegal, and when the bears eventually become a nuisance, the end result is often the death of bears.

Supervised bear-viewing programs, such as those at McNeil River State Game Sanctuary, Pack Creek on Admiralty Island, and Brooks River in Katmai National Park, offer excellent opportunities to observe bears at close range. Bears concentrate in all three of these areas to feed on salmon. You can learn a lot about bears and bear behavior by spending a few days at one of these sites and listening to personnel who are responsible for managing them. A number of private lodges, camps, boats, and air operators in coastal Alaska also offer guided bear-viewing services.

A good pair of binoculars, a spotting scope, or a telephoto lens makes it possible to watch and photograph the animals without getting too close. It is easiest to observe bears while they are fishing for salmon. Knolls or hills along streams provide excellent vantage points from which to watch them without disturbing their fishing.

It is more difficult to view bears when they are grazing in meadows. I frequently worked with bears in open meadows or digging clams on a tidal flat. Sometimes fifteen or twenty bears were visible, but scattered over a wide area. It is more difficult in this situation to get within range to photograph the animals without disturbing them, and I use the following approach. I keep my group close together and we walk slowly toward the bear we wish to photograph. I make sure that the animal sees us before we get closer than 150 to 200 yards. When the bear looks in our direction, I observe its reactions. Is it

nervous or is it comfortably continuing to feed? I might watch the animal for quite a while and if it remains calm and content, we move slowly forward at an angle toward the bear until we are in photographic range. If a bear acts nervous, we do not hesitate to back off and try another one.

Taking your time is very important. Do not make any sudden moves or loud noises. Be consistent with your approach. I prefer to circle slowly in front of a bear and let it feed toward me. This is the least disturbing approach because the bear can select its own range of tolerance. Most bears have a personal distance at which they become uncomfortable and leave. So do I: if one intrudes into my zone of comfort, I slowly back off. You should always give bears plenty of space. If they decide to move past you to feed or drink water, back away and give them plenty of room to pass.

If you see a group of photographers watching a bear, do not approach the animal from the opposite direction. This is not only unethical, but can be dangerous. Your approach might cause the bear to move too close to the first group.

When you work with a group of bears day after day, eventually they become tolerant and accepting of your presence. Those that do are referred to as "conditioned" bears or "habituated" bears. Some bears, however, never do learn to accept people. Perhaps they have had a bad experience or are unusually shy. Let them be.

As proper guests in bear country, we have the opportunity to observe the actions and behaviors of a beautiful and majestic animal in its natural surroundings. Few encounters in our lifetimes can equal this thrilling experience. We must remember, however, that we are the visitors. Our responsibility lies in respecting the rights of the bears in their wilderness home.

FIGURE 56   *Brown bears require large tracts of wilderness to survive, such as this lush feeding ground in Katmai National Park.*

15

ROOM TO ROAM

LOW FOG AND INCESSANT RAIN OBSCURED THE OLD-*growth rain forest that covers Chichagof Island in Southeast Alaska. The tops of the tall spruce and hemlock trees appeared like gray ghosts as they swayed in the strong winds that blew across from Chatham Strait. Through the foggy mists an old female brown bear with a young yearling cub emerged, following a bear trail that had been used for hundreds of years by thousands of bears. The family plodded methodically along the trail that wound through a jungle of devil's club and huckleberry thickets.*

She and her lone cub had spent the winter in a rock den high in the alpine regions of the island. After emerging from hibernation, they descended to some open avalanche slopes to forage on new shoots of sedges and various roots they dug out of the ground. As the summer progressed, they moved on to the green alpine sedge meadows. In July the sow led her cub down to the ocean beach where they feasted on the many salmon that were spawning in the myriad streams and rivers that flowed out of the mountains. The family traveled from drainage to drainage as the fish runs waxed and waned, often competing with other bears that were fishing the same rivers.

Now in late August, as the fish supply diminished in these drainages, the sow decided to travel to another bay. She knew from experience that it harbored a late run of chum salmon. She and the cub needed to feed on the fall run to gain the fat reserves that would sustain them through the coming winter of hibernation. As they moved through the forest, a few Sitka deer bounded from the trail and red squirrels chattered from tree trunks. The trail zigzagged up a precipitous slope that topped out at two thousand feet above the sea. The next valley was familiar to the old sow, as she had fished its major stream each fall for the past fifteen years. She eagerly anticipated the fish meals that would soon be available.

As the bear family reached a small knoll, the sow paused abruptly. The cub sensed that its mother had detected something unusual, and it rose to its hind legs to look, its front paws balanced on her back. The pair stood silently for some moments, peering into the rainy mists. Faint noises rose from the valley below. The sow cocked her head and sniffed the air, but did not recognize the strange sounds that now crescendoed. The mother and cub moved forward another hundred yards and found themselves at the edge of a huge clearing. The giant trees that had always been there now lay scattered and tangled on the ground. About two hundred feet ahead, a wide, barren gravel trail wound down toward the sea. The old brownie could not comprehend that, in the year since her last visit, a logging crew had pushed a road into the valley and was now in the process of clear-cutting the entire drainage.

As the mother and cub sat at the edge of the clearing, thoroughly perplexed, the distant sounds of chainsaws and Caterpillar tractors filled the air, sounds that she had never heard before. A large logging truck loomed out of the fog, its powerful diesel engine ripping apart the wilderness silence. At the same moment a gust of wind brought the scent of humans to her keen nostrils. This she had smelled before and had learned to fear from previous encounters. Suddenly every strange thing she saw and heard she associated with the alarming scent—the roaring truck, the hum of chainsaws, and the butchered forest. The old female knew she wanted no part of this frightening and alien scene. She whirled around and galloped back up the trail, scared and confounded, followed by her lone cub. They would be deprived of the late run of salmon and would have to survive on berries, now ripening on the higher mountain slopes, until they entered their den. A lean winter lay ahead.

The brown bear is a large and long-lived animal that requires large tracts of wild lands to meet its biological needs. It stands at the very peak of the animal kingdom in Alaska; only man can topple it off that perch. Will it survive the changes that have now been set in motion in many regions of Alaska, or will it go the way of the grizzly in the western United States and the brown bear of Europe? There too the great bear once roamed abundantly supreme until modern man appeared on the same scene. The bears were ruthlessly slaughtered and their habitat was destroyed; now only remnant populations remain in small sections of the western United States and in the remote mountains of Europe. In most areas their survival hangs by a thread.

In our day of modern technology, scientific knowledge, and environmental awareness, do we have the will and the foresight to assure perpetuation of this noble and symbolic animal for generations to come? Are we willing to make some economic sacrifices to assure survival of the brown and grizzly bears throughout much of Alaska? Or will future generations only dream and read about the great bears that once thrived in this great land?

If someone suddenly shot and killed half of the coastal brown bears in Alaska, people would rise up in arms. But subtle habitat deterioration, which is a slower process that is less noticed, may be having *the very same effect* over several generations. Apparently people are capable of measuring and recognizing the ecological changes that occur only within their short lifetimes. I have often wondered what Lewis and Clark would think if they could retrace their journey through the West today and see the changes that humans have wrought. They would be astounded, and I suspect Sacagawea would leave a trail of tears from the prairies to the sea.

I have been in Alaska only fifty years, yet the changes that have occurred during my sojourn here are striking and seem to be intensifying. When I arrived in 1951 in the southeastern part of the state, Alaska was a territory. The Ketchikan Pulp Mill was still under construction. Old-growth rain forest stretched along the mainland coast and over every island. The dense growths remained basically as they had existed for eons. Little could I realize that, in a few decades, much of the area would be clear-cut and roads would crisscross the islands where I was walking and exploring.

A few years later, when I moved to Kodiak Island, I felt reassured that two-thirds of the island had been set aside as a wildlife refuge for bears. I could not anticipate that twenty years later Congress would deed the heart of the refuge into private hands. I could not visualize that a major hydroelectric development would be constructed within a refuge that I had thought was forever wild. I could not foresee that much of the adjacent Afognak Island, a national forest, would also become private, with large portions clear-cut and interlaced with roads.

Throughout Alaska, changes are occurring at an accelerating rate. Alaska is rich in natural resources that are being extracted on a large scale. Oil discoveries led to the construction of the 800-mile pipeline and its access road, which bisects Alaska from the Arctic Ocean to the Gulf of Alaska. The population of 150,000 in the 1950s has now increased to more than 600,000. Tourists come by the thousands each year.

This expanding human population, coupled with modern transportation, has allowed hunters to penetrate formerly inaccessible regions of Alaska, fishermen and rafters to explore the last remote rivers, and hikers to enter pristine and wild mountain valleys. Wildlife viewers and photographers search out concentrations of bears in every secluded niche of Alaska. Those who have limited time can charter aircraft to observe bears.

To accommodate all these changes, new towns have sprung up and roads are being constructed; camps, lodges, and cabins dot the shorelines of the most isolated rivers, lakes, and seashores. We would be naive to think that Alaska has reached its peak population, that no more oil will be discovered and extracted, that the rich mineral resources will not be further exploited, that commercial logging will suddenly cease, or that fewer tourists and travelers will enter the last remote parts of the state. All these changes and human pressures have and will continue to have a cumulatively negative effect on the wilderness of Alaska and on all the bears that dwell therein.

Yes, brown bears have survived many of the developments and human population pressures, but they are likely to be greatly reduced or exterminated from many areas. Are we going to be satisfied with only a few bears in Alaska, or are we going to demand that in certain regions of this great state we will manage the wild lands in such a manner that bears will continue to thrive in their natural and historic numbers? One may appreciate the sight of a single brown bear, but an aggregation of bears in the great Alaskan wilderness is an awesome scene.

Fortunately, the conservation movement came to Alaska about the same time that rapid economic changes were unfolding. Before large oil and mineral extractions began and before the extensive transfer of federal lands into private hands, conservation groups demanded that a portion of the wild lands that once covered the entire state would be set aside forever. Those of us who saw the changes coming fought hard to establish large tracts of wilderness. Many of these areas preserved

in the coastal portions of Alaska contain some of the densest brown bear populations in the world. Here we have an excellent opportunity to shelter brown bears in historic numbers.

The region with perhaps the most prolific population of coastal brown bears is the expanse of wilderness that stretches from Kamishak Bay southwest to Kujulik Bay along the Alaska Peninsula. This area includes all the lands and waters within the McNeil River State Game Sanctuary and State Game Refuge, Katmai National Park and Preserve, Becharof National Wildlife Refuge, the Ugashik Unit of the Alaska Peninsula National Wildlife Refuge, and the Aniakchak Crater National Monument. Combined, these five natural conservation units encompass approximately ten thousand square miles, an area the size of Vermont. This vast land has a rich supply of salmon resources, lush vegetation, mountains, scenic vistas, and wilderness; it is extensive enough to form a complete ecosystem. By and large it is free of roads and human settlements and protected from harmful resource developments. It has all the ingredients for maintaining the large number of brown bears it now harbors.

Since these five conservation units were established, conservation groups and resource managers have been complacent in the belief that brown bears will thrive there forever. But again, forces are at work that could have detrimental effects on the bears and on the wild lands that they occupy in the future.

Suddenly everyone loves the brown bear. Bear viewers and photographers are flocking into these remote lands in ever-increasing numbers. Air operators from King Salmon, Kodiak, Homer, and other towns are transporting people into the region by the thousands. Vessels operate along the coast shuttling people ashore to observe bears and other wildlife. More than two hundred people each day fly into Brooks Camp during the busy summer tourist season, jamming the bear-viewing platforms and trails along the Brooks River, primarily to watch bears fishing for salmon. The Alaska Department of Fish and Game has long limited the number of visitors to the McNeil River Sanctuary to ten per day during the bear fishing season, but the number of applicants has risen rapidly; now only a small percentage of those applying are selected.

People want to see brown bears in the wild; this is good because these same people constitute an economic and ethical incentive to preserve bears. Yet as more and more tourists arrive land managers are pressured to provide facilities in the form of lodges, back-country cabins, campgrounds, trails, roads, and easier access sites, all of which encroach on the bears' territory. Tourism is big business in Alaska and many resource managers and business and political leaders make decisions based strictly on economic gains. They readily sacrifice wildlife and wilderness values to accomplish financial goals.

The welfare of the brown bear and its environment must be prioritized in this region if we are to perpetuate the dense population of bears and their ecosystem. The political will that created the conservation units demonstrates a clear mandate. We must enact a comprehensive management plan, encompassing the entire geographic area, in which the major goal will be the protection of wildlife and wilderness values for the long-term future. We must not permit economic developments that will seriously impact the ecosystem. Just as managers try to train bears to stay out of critical human zones around lodges and campgrounds, we must make some critical bear zones off-limits to people.

Many backcountry hikers, bear viewers, and nature photographers believe that their impact on the environment is negligible when they penetrate the last remote regions of the bears. By contrast, when a single bear injures a single human, people demand the removal of the animal. The ultimate result is as direct and dire as if a hunter had taken that bear.

It is important to have established areas such as Brooks Camp where large numbers of people can view and enjoy bears. These sites should be limited in number and chosen very carefully. We need innovative methods to permit people to see bears without crowding bears out of the region. These limits need to be established before areas are populated; implementing reforms after the carrying capacity of the ecosystem has been exceeded is politically difficult, if not impossible.

In other coastal regions in Alaska we still have the opportunity to maintain brown bear populations in historic numbers. The Kodiak National Wildlife Refuge, encompassing about two-thirds of Kodiak Island, was established for the major purpose of protecting the 2,500 or so bears within its massive landscape. The area has long been recognized as one of the premier brown bear ecosystems in the world. The seashore serves as a natural boundary, and the extensive fishery resources and lush coastal vegetation provide a bountiful food supply. Mountains and wild lands provide the other essential ingredients for a healthy brown bear utopia.

Conservationists were worried when Congress deeded large sections of critical bear habitat within the reserve to various villages and Native corporations under the 1971 Alaska Native Claims Settlement Act. However, conservation agencies cooperated with Native peoples and other island residents to restore many of these lands to the refuge. The larger tracts of lands were purchased with funds provided by the Exxon Valdez oil spill settlement fund (monies set aside by Exxon to mitigate damages caused by the 1989 oil spill). The Kodiak Brown Bear Trust (created as part of the Terror Lake hydro settlement) worked with various interest groups to purchase and restore many of the smaller tracts and private inholdings to the reserve. The Kodiak National Wildlife Refuge has once again become a shelter where brown bears can be sustained in perpetuity. Now we must have the will and foresight to establish and enforce regulations that will guarantee the long-term health of the brown bear population.

We must also continue the biological research that has been ongoing on the island for many years. These long-term studies provide important information on the life history of these remarkable animals and of the impacts that occur when people invade their environment.

The rain forests of Southeast Alaska on Chichagof, Baranof, and Admiralty islands have long sustained dense populations of brown bears. Large-scale commercial logging, with its vast clearcuts and network of roads on northern Baranof and eastern Chichagof islands, has seriously eroded this habitat and jeopardized the future of the bears that flourish there. The human activity that follows roads will surely bring increased conflict with the bears, fragmenting their habitat and greatly reducing their numbers. Hopefully, the citizens of Alaska will demand that at least a portion of these islands be protected from logging and perhaps restored to conditions that will allow the bears to endure the incursion of man.

The 1,709-square-mile Admiralty Island, with its 1,500 to 1,700 bears, is a haven for the animals. There, man and bear have long coexisted, both thriving on the rich salmon resources that migrate through the numerous saltwater bays and up the freshwater streams each summer. This vast expanse of old-growth rain forest was once slated to be logged by the U.S. Forest Service, but the residents of Angoon and other conservationists demanded that most of Admiralty Island be designated a national monument. In 1980, under the Alaska National Interest Lands Conservation Act (ANILCA), Congress protected much of it as wilderness. The island provides the best opportunity to maintain a dense population of brown bears in the rain forests of Southeast Alaska for the long-term future.

There are other areas in Alaska where we could conserve the present bear populations for posterity. But will we?

Perhaps I have painted an alarming picture for the future of brown bears in coastal Alaska. History, however, has shown that increasing human populations and resource development within brown bear or grizzly bear habitat does gradually reduce or eliminate the animals from their ranges. People and brown bears tend not to coexist very well. I see these forces at work in Alaska, as oil drilling, mining, logging, agriculture, road building, and recreational use gradually infringe on the environment of brown bears. Directly or indirectly, these activities do reduce bear numbers.

A case in point is the Kenai Peninsula, where I live. Biologists estimate that 250 to 300 brown bears inhabit this region. Their historical travel routes and feeding sites are now interwoven with highways, hiking trails, logging roads, and numerous rural cabins, homes, and subdivisions. The bears have difficulty following their traditional seasonal routes without coming into conflict with man, and each year an increasing number of them are killed in self-defense. In 1998, the Alaska

Department of Fish and Game listed the peninsula brown bears as a population of special concern. Will they survive the onslaught? Is this a prelude to what will happen to other brown and grizzly bear populations in Alaska?

I hope Alaskans and other U.S. citizens will demand that, in regions such as the Alaska Peninsula, Kodiak Island, and Admiralty Island, the government protect wilderness resources so that brown bears can thrive in abundance. We must draw the battle lines now and not retreat. We cannot let resource developers set the standards and still expect bears to survive in the wild. Viewing remnants of these animal populations in zoos or fenced enclosures may be good enough for some people, but it is not good enough for me.

Brown bears and grizzlies are among the most majestic wild animals that live in North America. In Alaska, these giant bears symbolize the lofty mountains, smoking volcanoes, ancient glaciers, vast wilderness, and scenic grandeur that define the great state. If the bears disappear from these lands, then we as humans have seriously failed in our stewardship of this earth.

REFERENCES

Atwell, G., D. L. Boone, J. Gustafson, and V. D. Berns. 1980. Brown Bear Summer Use of Alpine Habitat on the Kodiak National Wildlife Refuge. In *Bears—Their Biology and Management: A Selection of Papers from the Fourth International Conference on Bear Research and Management*, Kalispell, Montana, February 1977, edited by C. J. Martinka and K. L. McArthur, pp. 297–305. Bear Biology Association.

Aumiller, L. D., and C. Matt. 1994. Management of McNeil River State Game Sanctuary for Viewing of Brown Bears. In *Bears—Their Biology and Management: A Selection of Papers from the Ninth International Conference on Bear Research and Management*, Missoula, Montana, February 1992, edited by J. J. Claar, P. Schullery, L. J. Lyon, M. R. Johnson, and C. Servheen, pp. 51–61. International Association for Bear Management and Research.

Barnes, V. G. 1990. The Influence of Salmon Availability on Movements and Range of Brown Bears on Southwest Kodiak Island. In *Bears—Their Biology and Management: A Selection of Papers from the Eighth International Conference on Bear Research and Management*, Victoria, British Columbia, February 1989, edited by L. M. Darling, W. R. Archibald, and C. D. Frederick, pp. 305–313. International Association for Bear Management and Research.

Barnes, V. G, R. B. Smith, and L. G. Van Daele. 1988. Density Estimates and Estimated Population of Brown Bears on Kodiak and Adjacent Islands. Unpublished report submitted to the Kodiak Brown Bear Restoration and Habitat Maintenance Trust, Kodiak, Alaska.

Bledsoe, T. 1975. The Social Life of an Unsociable Giant. *Audubon* 17(3):2–16.

———. 1987. *Brown Bear Summer*. New York: E. P. Dutton.

Burkholder, R. L. 1951. Bear-Cattle Relationships on Kodiak Island. Unpublished report prepared for the United States Fish and Wildlife Service, Kodiak Refuge Files.

Clark, W. K. 1957. Seasonal Food Habits of the Kodiak Bear. *Transactions of the North American Wildlife Conference* 22:145–9.

———. 1959. Kodiak Bear–Red Salmon Relationships at Karluk Lake, Alaska. *Transactions of the North American Wildlife Conference* 24:337–345.

Eide, S. 1965. The Nature of Brown Bear Predation on Cattle, Kodiak Island, Alaska. *Proceedings of the Annual Conference of the Western Association of State Fish and Game Commissioners* 45:113–118.

Elliott, H. W. 1886. *Our Arctic Province: Alaska and the Seal Islands*. New York: C. Scribner's Sons.

Gabrielson, I. N. 1951. Crisis for Alaskan Wildlife. *Audubon* 53(6):348–353, 394–395.

Gard, R. 1971. Brown Bear Predation on Sockeye Salmon at Karluk Lake, Alaska. *Journal of Wildlife Management* 35(2):193–204.

Georgeson, C. C. 1929. Brief History of Cattle Breeding in Alaska. *United States Department of Agriculture Bulletin* 8, Washington, DC.

Glenn, L. P. 1980. Morphometric Characteristics of Brown Bears on the Central Alaska Peninsula. In *Bears—Their Biology and Management: A Selection of*

Papers from the Fourth International Conference on Bear Research and Management, Kalispell, Montana, February 1977, edited by C. J. Martinka and K. L. McArthur, pp. 313–319. Bear Biology Association.

Glenn, L. P., J. W. Lentfer, J. B. Faro, and L. H. Miller. 1976. Reproductive Biology of Female Brown Bears (*Ursus arctos*), McNeil River, Alaska. In *Bears—Their Biology and Management: A Selection of Papers from the Third International Conference on Bear Research and Management*, edited by M. R. Pelton, J. W. Lentfer, and G. E. Folks, pp. 381–390. Bear Biology Association.

Glenn, L. P., and L. H. Miller. 1980. Seasonal Movements of an Alaska Peninsula Brown Bear Population. In *Bears—Their Biology and Management: A Selection of Papers from the Fourth International Conference on Bear Research and Management*, Kalispell, Montana, February 1977, edited by C. J. Martinka and K. L. McArthur, pp. 307–312.

Herrero, S. 1985. *Bear Attacks, Their Causes and Avoidance*. Piscataway, NJ: Winchester Press.

Herrero, S., and A. Higgins. 1998. Field Use of *Capsicum* Spray as a Bear Deterrent. *Ursus* 10:533–537.

Holzworth, J. M. 1930. *The Wild Grizzlies of Alaska*. New York: Putnam & Sons.

Klein, D. R. 1965. Post Glacial Distribution Patterns of Mammals in the Southern Coastal Regions of Alaska. *Arctic* 18(1):7–20.

Lentfer, J. W., R. Hensel, L. H. Miller, L. P. Glenn, and V. D. Berns. 1972. Remarks on Denning Habits of Alaska Brown Bears. In *Bears—Their Biology and Management: A Selection of Papers from the Second International Conference on Bear Research and Management*, Calgary, Alberta, November 1970, edited by S. Herrero, pp. 125–137. Bear Biology Association.

Mathisen, O. A. 1962. The Effect of Altered Sex Ratios on the Spawning of Red Salmon. In *Studies of Alaska Red Salmon*, edited by T. S.-Y. Koo, pp. 137–222. Seattle: University of Washington Press.

Meehan, W. R. 1961. Observations on Feeding Habits and Behavior of Grizzly Bears. *American Midland Naturalist* 65(2):409–412.

Merrell, T. R. 1964. Ecological Studies of Sockeye Salmon and Related Limnological and Dematological Investigations, Brooks Lake, Alaska, 1957. United States Fish and Wildlife Service Special Scientific Report, *Fisheries* 456.

Miller, S. D., and W. B. Ballard. 1982. Homing of Transplanted Alaska Brown Bears. *Journal of Wildlife Management* 46(4):869–876.

Mundy, K. R. D., and W. Fuller. 1964. Age Determination in the Grizzly Bear. *Journal of Wildlife Management* 28(4):863–866.

Palmer, L. J. 1938. Wildlife Problems on Kodiak Island. Unpublished Special Report for the Alaska Game Commission, Juneau, AK.

Rausch, R. L. 1953. On the Status of Some Arctic Mammals. *Arctic* 6(2):91–148.

———. 1963. Geographic Variation in Size in North American Brown Bear *Ursus arctos* L. as Indicated by Condylobasal Length. *Canadian Journal of Zoology* 41:33–45.

Rearden, J. 1964. The Kodiak Bear War. *Outdoor Life* 134(2):17–19, 70–76.

Russell, A. 1979. *Grizzly Country*. New York: Alfred A. Knopf.

Sarber, H. 1939. Kodiak Brown Bear Control Project, Kodiak Island, Alaska. Unpublished Report for the Alaska Game Commission, Juneau, AK.

Schoen, J. W. 1990. Bear Habitat Management: A Review and Future Perspective. In *Bears—Their Biology and Management: A Selection of Papers from the Eighth International Conference on Bear Research and Management*, Victoria, British Columbia, February 1989, edited by L. M. Darling, W. R. Archibald, and C. D. Frederick, pp. 143–154. Bear Biology Association.

Schoen, J. W., L. R. Bier, J. W. Lentfer, and L. J. Johnson. 1987. Denning Ecology of Brown Bears on Admiralty and Chichagof Islands. In *Bears—Their Biology and Management: A Selection of Papers from the Seventh International Conference on Bear Research and Management*, Williamsburg, Virginia, February 1986, edited by P. E. Zager, J. Beecham, G. Matula, and H. V. Reynolds, pp. 293–2304. Bear Biology Association.

Schoen, J. W., J. W. Lentfer, and L. Bier. 1986. Differential Distribution of Brown Bears on Admiralty Island, Southeast Alaska: A Preliminary Assessment. In *Bears—Their Biology and Management: A Selection of Papers from the Sixth International Conference on Bear Research and Management*, Grand Canyon, AZ, February 1983, edited by P. E. Zager and D. L. Garshells, pp. 1–5. Bear Biology Association.

Schoen, J. W., S. B. Miller, and H. V. Reynolds, III. 1987. Last Stronghold of the Grizzly. *Natural History* 96:50–60.

Sellers, R. A., S. D. Miller, T. S. Smith, and R. Potts. 1993. Population Dynamics and Habitat Partitioning of a Naturally Regulated Brown Bear Population on the Coast of Katmai National Park. 1993 Annual Progress Report of the Alaska Department of Fish and Game, Juneau, AK.

Sellers, R. A., and L. D. Aumiller. 1994. Brown Bear Population Characteristics at McNeil River, Alaska. In *Bears—Their Biology and Management: A Selection of Papers from the Ninth International Conference on Bear Research and Management*, Missoula, Montana, February 1992, edited by J. J. Claar, P. Schullery, L. J. Lyon, M. R. Johnson, and C. Servheen, pp. 283–293. Bear Biology Association.

Schuman, R. F. 1950. Bear Depredations on Red Salmon Spawning Populations in the Karluk River System, 1947. *Journal of Wildlife Management* 14(1):1–9.

Stonorov, D. 2000. *Living in Harmony with Bears*. Anchorage, AK: Audubon Alaska, National Audubon Society.

Stonorov, D., and A. Stokes. 1972. Social Behavior of Alaskan Brown Bear. In *Bears—Their Biology and Management: A Selection of Papers from the Second International Conference on Bear Research and Management*, Calgary, Alberta, November 1970, edited by S. Herrero, pp. 232–42. Bear Biology Association.

Troyer, W. A. 1980. Movements and Dispersal of Brown Bear at Brooks River, Alaska. Unpublished Report for the National Park Service, Anchorage, AK.

Troyer, W. A., and J. Faro. 1975. Aerial Survey of Brown Bear Denning in the Katmai Area, Alaska. Unpublished Report for the National Park Service, Anchorage, AK.

Troyer, W. A., and R. J. Hensel. 1962. Cannibalism in Brown Bears. *Animal Behavior* 10:3–4.

———. 1964a. Behavior of Female Brown Bears Under Stress. *Journal of Mammalogy* 45(3):488–9.

———. 1964b. Structure and Distribution of a Kodiak Bear Population. *Journal of Wildlife Management* 28(4):769–772.

———. 1969. The Brown Bear of Kodiak Island. U.S. Bureau of Sport Fisheries and Wildlife.

Troyer, W. A., R. J. Hensel, and K. E. Durley. 1962. Live-trapping and Handling of Brown Bear. *Journal of Wildlife Management* 26(3):330–1.

Van Daele, L. J., 2003. *The History of Bears on the Kodiak Archipelago*. Anchorage: Alaska Natural History Association.

Van Daele, L. J., V. G. Barnes, and R. B. Smith. 1990. Denning Characteristics of Brown Bears on Kodiak Island, Alaska. In *Bears—Their Biology and Management: A Selection of Papers from the Eighth International Conference on Bear Research and Management*, Victoria, British Columbia, February 1989, edited by L. M. Darling, W. R. Archibald, and C. D. Frederick, pp. 257–67. Bear Biology Association.

Walker, T. 1993. *River of Bears*. Stillwater, MN: Voyageur Press.

INDEX

113, 118, 119
Meehan, W. R., 78
Merrell, Ted, 78
Merriam, C. Hart, 2
Miller, Lee, 44
Miller, Sterling, 44
mining, 120

N

National Park Service, 96, 103, 110–11
nursing, *37*, 37–39, *38*

O

oil drilling, 117, 118, 120
Ostermick, Rollie, 105

P

Pack Creek bear-watching camp, 113
pepper spray, 106–107
phenobarbital sodium, 94
play, *64*, 65–69, *68*
population. *See* distribution, of brown bear
population decline
    bear, 63, 77–79, 82
    salmon, 77–79
    See also bear-cattle war, Kodiak Island
predators
    control and destruction of, xii, 44, 77, 79, 84-87
    brown bear as, 73–79, 106
    See also bear-cattle war, Kodiak Island; charging
prey. *See* food sources; predators

R

radio collar, 96, 97, 105
range. *See* home range, of individual bears; distribution, of brown bears
Rausch, Robert L., 2–3
razor clam, *xiv*, 50, *52*, 53–54
Rearden, Jim, 86
research, biological. *See* trapping, for biological study
red salmon fishery, 12
resting/sleeping habits, 70, *71*. *See also* hibernation

Reynolds, Julius, 44
rubbing, 6, 7

S

salmon, 10, 12, 15, 51, 55, 57
    population decline, 77–78
    See also salmon fishing
salmon fishing, by bears
    competition in, *24*, 28, 30, 51
    sow and cubs, 25–26
    technique, 51, 53, *72*
sand lance, 54
Sarber, Hosea, 83
scat, 53, 54
Schoen, John, 51
Schuman, Richard, 77–78
Sellers, Dick, 39
sensory perception, 70–71, *71*
Sernylan, 96
shedding, 6, 7
siblings, 28, 65–66. *See also* cubs; play
size, of brown bears
    adult, 19, *20*, 21, 57
    calculating growth rate, 21
    calculating size, 21–23, *22*, 94
    female vs. male, 18–19
    newborn, 18, *19*, 37
    skull growth, 21
    three-year-old male, 21
    variation in, 22
    yearling cubs, 18, *20*
skull, 21
    used for classification, 2, *3*
smell, sense of, 70–71
Smith, Roger, 61
social life
    in crowded conditions, 20, 28
    hierarchy, 28, 30
    solitary, 26–27, 31
    of breeding pairs, 28, 36
    of adult males and cubs, 31
    play, *64*, 65–69, *68*
    of siblings, 28
    of sows and cubs, 26–28, 30, 37–39, 54
    See also aggression; cubs; male bears, behavior
Spencer, Dave, 85
succinylcholine, 94

survival, of brown bear, 115–121
    biological research and, 120
    conservation efforts, 84, 85, 86, 118–20
    effect of development on, 117, 118, 119, 120
    effect of tourism on, 117–119
    See also human impacts on brown bears; population decline
swimming ability, *42*, 43, 44, 69–70

T

Talifson, Morris, 67, 69
taxidermy, 4
taxonomy, 3
tooth rings, using for aging bears, 21
tourism in bear country, 87, 110–13, 118–119
    bear-watching camps, 110–111, *111*, *112*, 113
    injuries, rarity of, 110, 111
    photography, *108*, *112*, 113
    safety advice, 105-106, 110–111
tracks, calculating bear size from, 21–22, *22*
trapping, for biological study, xiii, 89–97
    cubs, 92–93, 95
    culvert trap, 90–91, *91*
    darting, 96–97
    double-spring steel trapping, *92*, 92–94
    drugs for subduing, 94, 96
    use of ether, 90, 91–92
    foot snare, 31, *91*, 92, 94
    pioneer work in, xiii, 89–94, 95
    processing bear after, 97
    safer/more humane, 94–96
travel, brown bear, 12, 35, *40*, 41–47, *46*, 55, 86, 120. *See also* home range, of individual bears
travel, to bear country. *See* tourism in bear country
tree climbing, 69
trophy bear, 21, 22